# *The* Maple Leaf Entrepreneur's Guide to Selling Your Business

Jim Nairn, MBA, MCBI, BCA

Jim Nairn-- 1st ed.
Chief Editor, Shannon Buritz

ISBN: 978-1-954757-68-4

The Publisher has strived to be as accurate and complete as possible in the creation of this book.

This book is not intended for use as a legal, business, accounting, or financial advice source. All readers are advised to seek the services of competent professionals in legal, business, accounting, and finance fields.

Like anything else in life, there are no guarantees of income or results in practical advice books. Readers are cautioned to rely on their judgment about their individual circumstances to act accordingly.

While all attempts have been made to verify the information provided in this publication, the Publisher assumes no responsibility for errors, omissions, or contrary interpretations of the subject matter herein. Any perceived slights of specific persons, peoples, or organizations are unintentional.

*This book would not have been possible without the many amazing people in my personal and professional life. Their support, guidance, and encouragement have shaped my journey in countless ways.*

*On the professional side, I am deeply grateful to my business partner, Mr. John Patrick, whose guidance and support have helped me refine my skills, particularly when working with clients under challenging circumstances. I also want to recognize the incredible team within the Sunbelt Canada organization and the staff and members of the IBBA and M&A Source—their comradery, education, and insights have been invaluable.*

*On a personal level, my family has been my foundation. My mother has shown extraordinary strength and courage while battling serious health challenges this past year. Despite it all, she has maintained her cheery, upbeat disposition, and her resilience is truly inspiring.*

*Of course, none of this would be possible without the unwavering, unconditional love of my true partner in life, my confidant, and my ride-or-die, Linda. You are simply the best; my life would not be complete without you.*

*I cannot forget our incredible children. It has been an honor to watch them navigate life with perseverance and grace. I am eternally grateful for their love and support as I continue to grow in my life and career.*

*To each of you—thank you from the bottom of my heart.*

# Contents

Foreword ............................................................................. vii

Introduction ....................................................................... ix

CHAPTER 1   Preparing to Sell Your Business In Canada ............. 1

CHAPTER 2   From Emotion to Economics: Understanding
Business Value ..................................................... 13

CHAPTER 3   Maximizing Your Business Value After Taxes ....... 27

CHAPTER 4   Working Capital and Cash Flows ......................... 35

CHAPTER 5   Taxes .................................................................. 43

CHAPTER 6   Lawyers, Liabilities, and Legal Safeguards ............ 49

CHAPTER 7   Marketing Your Business ..................................... 67

CHAPTER 8   Confidentiality and Finding the Ideal Buyer ........ 75

CHAPTER 9   Buying a Business ................................................ 81

CHAPTER 10   After Selling Your Business ................................. 93

CHAPTER 11   The 30 Roles of a Business Broker ..................... 101

BONUS   Conversation with Grant Mellow ...................... 111

Epilogue ........................................................................... 117

About Jim Nairn, MBA, MCBI, BCA .................................... 121

What Jim's Clients Are Saying. ........................................... 123

# Foreword

I'm honoured to write a foreword for Jim Nairn's book on selling a business in Canada. This book is an invaluable guide for those selling the businesses they've built—often over decades of dedication. As an entrepreneur who has built a startup, acquired another business, and then successfully sold both, I understand both sides of the transaction.

What makes this book so valuable is its candor and practicality. It respects the emotional weight of letting go while grounding readers in the clear-eyed realities of valuation, timing, negotiation, and transition. It equips sellers with the knowledge to protect and maximize what they've built.

If you are preparing to sell your company, the insights here will help you navigate the process with clarity, respect, and purpose. It is more than a manual on transactions—it is a roadmap to preserving legacies and fostering the next step in your journey.

## Shari Hughson, RN, BScN, MBA
## 8X Serial Entrepreneur & Consultant

Shari is an 8X serial Entrepreneur and side-hustle educator at Queen's University, Canada, teaching in Innovation, Disruptive Technologies, Entrepreneurship, and social impact strategy for People and the Planet. Shari's enterprises have been in MedTech, EdTech, & Health. Shari bootstrapped one company and acquired another with VC support, building both to National scale before a successful exit (sale). She has also spent several years learning and building environmental innovations in housing, water management, and circular food systems, while living off the land for 7 years (TEDx). Shari currently has 2 passion project enterprises, as the co-founder, CEO/CFO of both Neuma Centre a global psychedelic consulting & education company, and AdventurePI, a company investigating mis-adventures in travel and the wilderness, learning from those who survived, those who didn't, and getting 'boots on the ground' for those still missing.

Shari started her first business in her 20s & won CIBC Entrepreneur of the Year before the age of 30. She recently won Canada's Top 50 Most Influential Business & Entrepreneur Female Leaders of the Year in 2021 by SME Canada. Shari is a sought after professional speaker, coach, & consultant for startup and scaleup entrepreneurs, sustainable development, and success mindset.

# Introduction

My hope is that this book will guide you to the ultimate success, which, after years of hard work, is enjoying a stress-free life after selling your business. You should be able to retire comfortably from the sale of your business after making sure that your employees, customers, and the relationships you've built are well taken care of. The ideal succession should seamlessly address all these aspects. In this book, I'll guide you through the process of selling your business in Canada, ensuring that your exit strategy is effective and aligns with your personal and financial goals.

Despite the benefits, you might wonder why you haven't achieved this ideal exit already. Many business owners I work with are too busy to plan or manage the sale of their business. While you may have considered selling, the daily demands of running your business have prevented you from devoting the necessary time to the process. Don't worry; this isn't unusual; your primary focus has been growing your business, not figuring out how to sell it.

Selling a business isn't something you do every day. The skills required to do this are typically not learned until the need arises. There's a good chance you might be unsure of what steps are involved, what needs to be prioritized, and when. Therefore, it's natural to feel unprepared when the time to sell approaches.

Quite often, the business owners I work with do not clearly understand what their business is truly worth from a market perspective. While you may have a deep sentimental attachment to your business, understanding its market value is entirely different.

Recognizing these challenges is the first step toward overcoming them. In the following chapters, I'll guide you through strategies so you can manage your time effectively, gain essential knowledge about the selling process, and understand the real market value of your business. This knowledge will empower you to approach the sale of your business with confidence and clarity.

One significant hurdle you might face is the fear of the unknown. This fear can manifest in various ways, but I've noticed a couple of common key concerns among business owners along the way.

First, you may worry about whether your business is sellable at all. This doubt can be paralyzing, making it difficult to take even the first steps toward preparing for a sale. The concern is about more than finding a buyer; it is about whether your business's structure and foundation hold enough value to attract serious interest.

Then, when a potential buyer examines every aspect of your business—financials, employee records, HR policies—you might worry about what they will find. Will they judge how you've been running things? Could there be deal-breakers hidden in your books?

These fears are valid, but they should not deter you. These challenges are manageable, and part of my role is to help you prepare and present your business in the best light possible, addressing any issues that could potentially derail prospective buyers. This preparation makes your business more attractive and helps alleviate the fear of the unknown by giving them a clear picture of your business's strengths and areas for improvement.

Unique characteristics of your business might seem like obstacles in attracting buyers or achieving a satisfactory sale. For example, you might worry about the perceived lack of demand for intellectual property-driven businesses like technical firms or highly specialized healthcare services. You might think, "Who would want to buy my specialized business?" or "Who is qualified to run it after me?" These concerns are also valid, as the pool of potential buyers who understand and value such businesses may seem smaller than more traditional ones. However, that doesn't mean that there aren't qualified buyers out there, your business could still be very salable.

Additionally, if you are the name and face of your business, you may worry about complicating the selling process. For instance, how does one transition "John Smith's Repair Shop" when John Smith himself is closely tied to the business identity? It might seem challenging, but it's not impossible. I've worked with businesses where the owner was significantly branded with the company, and we've managed successful transitions by carefully strategizing how to rebrand and reposition the business after the sale.

These unique attributes can also be selling points. For example, if your business is the sole supplier for a critical government need, this necessity can demonstrate the business's essential role and long-term viability. We can frame these unique elements as special features that offer hard-to-replicate value.

My goal is to help you turn these perceived challenges into opportunities. Later on, we'll explore how to do this and answer some of your most pressing questions about selling your business, including:

- *"How do I determine the value of my business?"*
- *"What steps should I take to prepare my business for sale?"*
- *"What is the process of selling a business in Canada?"*
- *"What are the legal and tax implications of selling my business?"*

- *"What role do business brokers play in the selling process?"*

Beyond these typical questions, you might have suspicions about the intentions of those helping you with the sale, particularly business brokers like me. Given the stakes involved, this is a natural concern, and it's important we address this head-on.

A common suspicion is that business brokers are primarily motivated by their commissions—that we are in it just for the money and not genuinely interested in your success or well-being. This skepticism can make you wary of seeking the help you truly need, potentially isolating you during a time when support is most crucial.

While business brokers, of course, earn a living from successful deals, the heart of our work is far from the cold transactional nature that these suspicions might suggest. For many of my respected colleagues and me, our primary goal is to safeguard your interests and ensure you achieve the best possible outcome when selling your business.

We strive not only to facilitate a sale but to do so in a way that respects and enhances your legacy. We do what we can to ensure that your business transitions smoothly so the new owner will continue building upon what you've created. My commitment is to provide a service that sees you comfortably onto your next chapter, whether in retirement, starting a new venture, or whatever you choose to pursue.

I have been involved in the business brokerage world for over a decade. This experience has equipped me with a thorough understanding of the market dynamics and the complexities of selling businesses across various industries. As part of my commitment to continuous learning, I'm one of the few people with the Master Certified Business Intermediary (MCBI) designation here in Canada. At the time that this book was published, I was the only business broker with this designation between Toronto and Montreal.

More importantly, my primary motivation is the success of your business transition. I understand that for many business owners, their company is their largest asset and a culmination of their life's work; there's often a significant emotional attachment to their business, and I don't blame them. My goal is to help you realize the wealth stored within your business and ensure that you receive the true value of your investment.

Success in selling your business can mean different things to different people. Certainly, the proceeds from the sale play a significant role, but the real value of success extends well beyond the financial aspects. What will those funds enable you to do next? How will they transform your life and allow you to pursue dreams that were once deferred due to the demands of running a business? Of course, we cannot forget about your staff, customers, suppliers, and other relationships you've formed over the years; those also need to be looked after.

The goals and aspirations can be as varied as the individuals themselves. Some of you might use the proceeds to buy another business, driven by the desire for new challenges and opportunities. Others may have dedicated decades to their business and now want a more relaxed pace of life. Retirement doesn't just mean stepping away from work; it's about enjoying time with family, traveling, exploring hobbies, giving back to the community with your time vs your money, and doing everything that there was never enough time for.

As we move forward in this book, think about what success means to you. What does it look like? What will be better in your life once you have successfully transitioned from your business? Let the answers to these questions guide your strategy as you prepare your business to go to market.

When I decided to write this book, my primary motivation was to extend my reach beyond the individual transactions I handle day-to-day and touch a broader audience of entrepreneurs. Many business owners are unaware of the full spectrum of support available beyond the conventional channels of lawyers and accountants. There is a significant educational component in what business brokers do—training and preparing you not just to sell your business but to understand the process deeply enough to feel empowered and confident. Through this book, I aim to raise awareness of this specialized support so you can achieve a transition that honors your journey of hard work and dedication as a business owner.

- Jim Nairn

CHAPTER

# PREPARING TO SELL YOUR BUSINESS IN CANADA

If you're even remotely considering selling your business, this chapter will give you a foundational understanding of what's required to set yourself up for success. One of the first questions I ask business owners contemplating a sale is why they want to sell and what do they plan to do afterward. The depth of their answers often indicates their level of preparedness. Some say, "I don't know...probably just do whatever I want." This response is too vague and suggests they haven't truly considered what life post-sale looks like. Quite often, it means that they aren't ready to sell their business.

Real readiness comes from detailed planning about life's next chapters. Whether coaching your grandkids' baseball team, spending more time at properties overseas, or relocating to be closer to family, having clear plans gives both of us confidence that you're ready for this significant change.

Financial readiness is equally important. Are you in touch with your financial advisor? Have you discussed your retirement goals and what it will take to achieve them? These conversations help determine if the timing is right for selling your business. If you haven't started this process, I can connect you with trusted professionals who can prevent you from "shooting in the dark;" instead, you can make well-informed decisions that align with your future goals.

## *Timing Is Everything*

As with any valuable asset, whether a classic car, an ancient coin, or a piece of prime real estate, the golden rule is to sell when the value peaks. This principle holds equally true for businesses. Selling your business when it's thriving—when sales and profits are at their highest—more often than not, ensures you can capitalize on its maximum market value. This timing attracts more buyer interest and typically results in a better sale price.

However, life doesn't always allow for ideal timing. Sometimes, business owners come to see me after experiencing one of the "Dismal Ds:" Death, Declining Sales, Disability, Dissolution, and Divorce. In these cases, the decision to sell might not align perfectly with the business's peak performance. Unfortunately, once a business has experienced one or more of these, its value is often not what it once was. Yet, under normal circumstances, without such pressures, the best time to sell is undoubtedly when your business shows strong, steady growth. If you have the capability, please don't wait to see me until after you've experienced one or more of the Dismal Ds!

From a valuation perspective, a business that has demonstrated consistent growth over the past five years is often at an optimal point to enter the market. This historical performance indicates to potential buyers that the business has a solid operational framework and is likely to continue prospering. Of course, there's no crystal ball to predict whether next year will bring better or worse conditions, but a track record of growth forms a compelling case for buyers.

## ENHANCING APPEAL

Even businesses that aren't in peak condition can still be made attractive to buyers. It's a common scenario—owners often decide to sell without the recommended three to five years of preparatory planning. They might say, "I need out now," for personal or professional reasons. Despite this urgency, many of these businesses are profitable and operational, which are appealing attributes for the right buyer.

When a business shows signs of a downturn in profitability or sales, it doesn't mean it's without potential. Some buyers specialize in turning around these businesses. They bring fresh energy and a new perspective that can revitalize the company's operations. My role is to connect these businesses with buyers who see beyond the current state and recognize the underlying value. These buyers typically have the expertise and drive needed to implement effective changes and capitalize on the business's strengths. One thing that you should know about these buyers is that, in this situation, they will not overpay for a business. If they need to put in the hard work to grow it, they will not be paying you extra just for the opportunity.

In fact, any price they offer will likely be discounted based on the amount of time and money they will need to invest in the business after closing.

However, there are limits to what can be done if a business is significantly underperforming or has been unprofitable for an extended period. In cases where a business is beyond feasible recovery, it might not be in the owner's best interest to seek a sale. Sometimes, the more practical option could be closing the business and liquidating assets through platforms like Kijiji or Facebook Marketplace. While it's a tough decision, this route might prevent further financial losses and allow the owner to recover some investment from the remaining tangible assets.

## Aligning Personal Goals with Business Sale Timing

The timeline for selling a business can vary—some sales wrap up within three months, while others can take anywhere from six to eighteen months or more. In some cases, businesses don't sell at all. This unpredictability makes it challenging to perfectly align the sale of your business with your personal goals and retirement plans.

Given the uncertainties, I advise planning for a sale within a one to two-year window. This approach allows business owners to be prepared if the sale concludes sooner than anticipated but also sets a realistic expectation for how long it might take.

Additionally, the timing of your sale might benefit from considering the business's seasonality. Selling during the off-season can allow the new owner to ramp up and prepare for the upcoming busy period. This strategic timing can make the business more attractive and streamline the transition for the new owner, aligning with their fiscal planning.

## *Emotional Attachments*

Selling a business is an emotional process that can impact your sense of identity and community presence. Many business owners are deeply connected to their business's role in the community—sponsoring events, supporting local charities, and being a visible part of local life. Realizing that these connections may diminish post-sale can lead to an identity crisis. "What's going to happen? Nobody will want to talk to me or shake my hand and ask how business is going?"

If you haven't considered your life after selling your business, you could be making it even harder on yourself. Planning for activities or roles you might take on post-sale can ease the emotional transition.

### EMOTIONS DURING NEGOTIATION

Emotions can reach an all-time high during negotiations. Sellers may feel their life's work is undervalued, leading to responses like, "Don't they realize that I put in 50 years of my life running my business, and they only want to give me this much for it?!"

Meanwhile, buyers seek to secure a deal that supports their future plans, often leading to conflicting motivations. From their point of view, they are thinking, "Why is the seller wanting too much of my money? Don't they know that I only have so much, and I'm already investing the majority of my (family's) life savings into this deal?!"

To manage these dynamics, I place myself between the buyer and seller, absorbing the negative emotions to keep negotiations professional and productive. This careful mediation helps both parties move forward successfully, setting the stage for collaboration during the crucial training and transition period post-sale. This is an important part of my job, as the buyer and seller usually need to work together, sometimes for up to two years or more, after closing. If those negative emotions are attached to the other party, that can make this period rather difficult and could cause the buyer to be unsuccessful in running the business.

## *Owner Readiness and Preparation*

The first step in selling your business is to talk with your financial advisor about your financial needs and goals post-sale, whether that is retiring, investing in another venture, or any other plans. Understanding what you need financially from the sale helps establish a target and decide if it's the right time to sell or focus on enhancing your business's value first.

Another key preparation involves your accountant. Many business owners in Canada manage their finances to optimize tax benefits. This often means the business's balance sheet includes personal investments like stocks, bonds, real estate, or even luxury items like boats or planes. These assets are usually not sold with the business and need careful handling for a tax-efficient transition.

Your accountant must strategize removing these assets from the business's books, which could involve transferring them to other holdings or directly to you. This process can be complex and time-consuming, potentially spanning two to three years, depending on the asset's nature and value. Planning this transfer early is vital to avoid financial penalties and to optimize the tax implications.

Real estate owned by the business but used for operations can also complicate the sale. If a potential buyer is interested only in the business and not the real estate, you may need to retain ownership of the property and lease it to the buyer. These decisions affect the business's balance sheet and have major tax and financial implications.

Understanding these scenarios in advance allows you to prepare adequately, ensuring you can navigate the complexities of the sale smoothly and efficiently. The goal is to minimize surprises and maximize your financial return by aligning the business's assets with your personal and financial aspirations.

## GETTING YOUR DUCKS IN A ROW

Having all documentation in place, such as employee job descriptions and standard operating procedure (SOP) manuals, is an excellent strategy for maximizing your business's value. These documents are crucial, especially in manufacturing or client services sectors, as they outline how tasks are performed and ensure consistency across operations. The presence of SOPs can enhance a buyer's confidence by demonstrating that the business operates efficiently and can be easily taken over post-sale. Documenting the main processes makes the training and transition much smoother.

Another aspect of readiness is keeping all administrative elements up-to-date. This includes maintaining current insurance on assets like vehicles and ensuring that all human resources requirements, such as workers' compensation claims, are settled. Often, older vehicles get abused, neglected, or are not used anymore, but owners are still paying insurance premiums on them. Handling these details prevents unnecessary costs and shows the buyer that you don't let any aspects of your business fall through the cracks.

Professional advisors are pivotal in assessing and enhancing a seller's readiness. They help organize and update the necessary documents and administrative details, ensuring the business is presented in the best possible light. Their expertise keeps everything from insurance to SOPs in order, streamlining the sale and potentially increasing the business's market value.

## *Reaping the Readiness Benefits*

One of my more memorable success stories is about an insulation business owner who was overwhelmed by the stress of managing his company. He was more hands-on than necessary, which only exacerbated his ongoing health issues. He was desperate for a change when he contacted me following one of my outreach campaigns. Luckily, we found a perfect buyer who owned complementary businesses in the area. This acquisition allowed the buyer to directly integrate our client's services, eliminating the need to contract outside companies.

Post-sale, the previous owner took the opportunity to relax and rejuvenate, spending the winter fishing in Florida. He shared photos of his new, stress-free life, standing on the beach with a cooler and his fishing rod, a huge contrast to his previous state. His transformation was so drastic that even his girlfriend noticed a change in his demeanor, remarking on how relaxed and easygoing he had become. This story highlights how selling a business can impact personal well-being when the timing is right.

Another example involves a friend who purchased a generator business from an owner ready to retire. The seller was a solo operator who had run the business for many years. Once the transition was complete, he didn't waste any time; he immediately started a new adventure, flying his plane around the world. Selling a business can provide liberation and freedom, especially for those who have dedicated many years to their enterprise.

A third case involved a young woman who owned a niche sporting goods store. Like the insulation business owner, she faced a lot of stress from managing her business, which affected her health and happiness. After we successfully closed the sale, she was able to move on and start a new venture in a totally unrelated field. While she still feels stressed when recalling her past business experiences, she is much happier now and enjoys her new life and business.

On the flip side, I've encountered situations where business owners were not ready to sell, sometimes leading to them closing their businesses entirely. Thankfully, these have been few and far between, but I mention them to remind you why your life's work deserves proper planning and readiness.

## *Committing to the Process*

It's important to recognize the level of commitment required from you, the business owner, throughout the process of selling your business. While I will take on much of the workload, you and your staff still need significant involvement. Your active participation is required, from accessing systems and files to gathering information for valuation, marketing, interviewing the prospective buyer(s), and negotiating a deal.

Selling your business is not just a transaction; it involves a fundamental shift in identity from being a business owner to embarking on new ventures. This transition requires a readiness to let go, which must be in place before reaching the final stages of a sale. Without this readiness, even the best deals will fall through at the last moment, wasting your time, money, and other resources as well as those of the buyer and the professionals involved, myself included.

As you consider selling your business, think of it as finishing a chapter in a book, with the next chapter ready to begin. You should be prepared emotionally, financially, and logistically for this change. This preparedness will help to ensure a smooth transition and allow you to fully embrace the next phase of your life with enthusiasm and confidence.

## KEY TAKEAWAYS

➢ Ensure personal and financial readiness before selling your business, considering your future goals and the optimal timing for market conditions.

➢ Prioritize selling your business when it demonstrates strong and consistent growth, as this can maximize market value and attract more buyers.

➢ Even businesses in less-than-ideal conditions can be appealing to the right buyers, especially those looking for turnaround opportunities.

➢ Address emotional attachments and plan for life post-sale to facilitate a smoother transition and reduce potential identity crises.

➢ Maintain detailed documentation and update all administrative elements to enhance business appeal and streamline the sale process.

CHAPTER

# FROM EMOTION TO ECONOMICS: UNDERSTANDING BUSINESS VALUE

Understanding the true worth of your business is a fundamental step, whether you're preparing to sell, resolving a partnership dispute, or planning for future growth. Over the years, I've worked with countless business owners, each with unique stories and emotional ties to their businesses. Many develop a deep emotional attachment after dedicating 20 to 30 years or more to their business. It's not just a business; it becomes like a family member; it's quite literally like their baby.

Owners often see their business through the lens of all the

sweat equity they have invested. This includes covering shifts for sick employees, repairing equipment during emergency breakdowns, and countless other sacrifices. This deep personal investment can lead them to believe their business is worth more than what anyone else would be willing to pay for it. It's not uncommon for someone who thinks their business should fetch two or three million dollars to discover its actual value is closer to $500,000. This emotional overestimation can lead to unrealistic expectations when it comes to selling.

Sentimental value does not translate well when selling your business. Potential buyers do not share the same history or emotional attachment. They focus on tangible aspects: the business's historical financial performance and potential for future growth. They're betting on what they can achieve with your business to ensure a good return on their investment that will support their family's future goals and dreams.

This disconnect between the seller's emotional valuation and what the market is willing to pay can be a stumbling block. I've seen this numerous times, particularly with family-owned businesses where years of hard work, personal sacrifices, and family legacy are on the line. One memorable case involved a business that was valued at around $750,000. Given this business's risk and other factors, we recommended listing it on the market at around $850,000. However, the owners were convinced their business was worth closer to $1.2 million, driven more by their emotional connection than market realities.

While the business had cash flow that could theoretically support an asking price of around $1.2 million, the market wouldn't bear it, given the inherent risks and specifics of that industry. The result was that the owner wasn't ready to go to market, mainly because they expected more. After some time, they returned and decided to proceed with the sale at the suggested price. This told me that they were finally ready to take the next steps.

Then there are those who aren't ready to face the facts. I've encountered business owners who, upon hearing a valuation they didn't like, would storm out, call me every name under the sun, and tell me how to conduct myself better. It's not the most pleasant part of the job, but it quickly shows me that they aren't ready to hear the truth about their business or move forward with the process. And honestly, I would rather find out in the early stages that someone's not truly ready to sell, versus going through the whole process only to find out at the very end that they aren't ready to move on.

Sometimes, I have to give advice that no one wants to hear— like suggesting that they might be better off selling their assets on platforms like Kijiji or through an auction rather than engaging a business broker like me. In some cases, this is simply the best route to obtain whatever value they can extract.

Being a "truth-teller" isn't the most enjoyable part of what I do, but it's essential. Business owners come to me for an honest assessment, and that's what I provide. Of course, they're always hoping for the best, and so am I. But there's only so much one can do; you can't make a business worth more than what it truly is. As the saying goes, "You can only put so much lipstick on a pig."

For business owners, it's crucial to separate emotional attachment from the hard realities of the market. Professional valuations help align expectations with market conditions, providing a clear path forward. Whether adjusting the asking price or considering alternative exit strategies, getting an honest, professional opinion ensures that you can make informed decisions in your best interest.

It's not always about selling the business for the highest price.

I've worked with business owners who were willing to accept a lower price because they felt that a particular buyer would be a better fit for their business, their staff, and their customers. To them, it was more about taking care of the people who've worked with them and helped them grow the business—they wanted to look after them and their families.

## *The Purpose of Valuation*

There are numerous reasons to get a business valuation, each requiring a different approach. For instance, a valuation for resolving a partner dispute differs from one prepared for going to market. Similarly, valuations for divorce settlements, tax, or a freeze on the business's value for future tax planning purposes each have unique requirements and results. You must get the correct type of valuation for the intended purpose.

A valuation method designed for tax disputes or CRA purposes can lead to inaccurate results when preparing to sell a business. These valuations may not highlight the factors a buyer would consider, such as future growth potential and market conditions. When preparing to sell, it is essential to work with someone who understands the specific needs of selling a business and what buyers are looking for.

In addition, the person you work with should have local or regional market knowledge. Many companies offer valuation services across different parts of Canada and the United States, but if they're not familiar with the local market where your business operates, the results can be significantly off. Local market conditions can play a significant role in determining the true value of a business. Using a valuation that doesn't account for these specifics can mislead you, impacting your strategy when selling your business.

Some companies can charge exorbitant fees—up to $50,000 or more—for a valuation. While it's important to invest in a proper valuation, ensuring you're getting value for your money is equally crucial. Overpaying for a valuation, especially if it doesn't meet the specific needs of your situation, can be a costly mistake. Seek out experienced professionals who offer fair pricing and deliver accurate, relevant valuations tailored to your business's needs.

## *How Market Conditions Impact Business Valuations*

When considering selling your business, it's crucial to understand how current market conditions, industry trends, and economic factors impact its valuation. One major factor is the fluctuation of interest rates. We experienced an unusually low interest rate environment for a period—rates hovering around 0% or just above, making borrowing almost feel like free money. It created an illusion that you could borrow as much as you wanted without much risk. However, as many of us who've been around the block a few times know, interest rates don't stay that low forever.

The Bank of Canada, like central banks elsewhere, makes quarterly decisions to adjust interest rates based on the state of the economy to keep inflation between 2% and 3%. Whether they succeed is up for debate, but their actions directly impact the affordability of loans for Canadians.When rates were low, individuals and businesses could afford more debt because the repayment costs were manageable. You saw folks taking out big mortgages and business loans because the monthly payments seemed reasonable.

However, things shift dramatically when interest rates climb. Recently, we've seen rates jump to 12% or even 13% in some cases. The difference in loan payments between borrowing at 2% versus 12% is staggering; the cost of servicing that debt becomes much higher. This directly impacts what buyers are willing—or able—to pay for your business.

Potential buyers often can't afford to borrow as much when interest rates are high. This means they're less likely to pay a premium price for a business. They either look to buy at a lower price or require the seller to provide more financing options. Seller financing often comes with more flexible repayment terms than banks, which are not known for their leniency. A seller might allow a buyer to make a reduced payment for one month, understanding that business ebbs and flows. In contrast, banks are typically more rigid and quicker to foreclose when there's a sign of trouble.

As a business owner looking to sell, it is beneficial to understand how macroeconomic factors can influence not only your business's value but also the deal's structure. Consider how flexible you'll need to be in financing a sale to make your business more attractive in a high-interest-rate environment.

## INDUSTRY TRENDS DRIVING BUSINESS SALES

Understanding industry trends is just as important as knowing the broader economic factors. Right now, consolidation is a significant trend across various industries. Take the medical field, for instance—whether it's dentistry, veterinary practices, orthotics, or physiotherapy, there's a surge in demand from companies looking to buy independent practices. These companies aim to consolidate their position in the market, and part of that strategy involves acquiring established businesses and gradually converting them to align with their existing brand or chain model.

The same pattern occurs in other professional services sectors, such as law firms and accounting practices. Companies want to build a stronger, more cohesive presence by bringing independently owned firms under their umbrella. The idea is to leverage the existing client base of these smaller firms, bringing their brand reputation and operational efficiency to strengthen their market presence.

Consolidation isn't confined to professional services or the medical field; it's happening almost everywhere. Even in sectors like floristry, you might find a local florist buying out competitors in their city to cement their market presence and open additional satellite offices. In construction, electrical companies often purchase smaller electrical businesses to gain access to their clients and skilled tradespeople, facilitating faster growth and expanding service offerings.

There is a significant opportunity for business owners across various regions, such as the Highway 401 corridor between Ottawa and Toronto. Many companies from Ottawa, Toronto, or even beyond—like the United States—are looking to establish a foothold in Ontario. These buyers are eager to expand their market reach and take on larger transactions. Acquiring an existing business rather than starting from scratch provides a faster route to market presence and growth.

If you own a business in an industry undergoing consolidation, this trend could present a substantial opportunity. Companies looking to expand their market share are sometimes willing to pay a premium for the right businesses that offer the strategic advantages they seek, whether that is an established customer base, a skilled workforce, and/or a desirable geographic location. As a seller, understanding this trend and positioning your business as a prime acquisition target could help you achieve a higher valuation and more favorable terms.

## *The Depth of Valuation*

A common challenge I encounter with business owners is their desire for a quick valuation. They often approach me with just a few years' earnings, expecting a rapid, definitive assessment of their business's value. However, the process is not that straightforward. Valuing a business requires meticulous and comprehensive analysis, not just a quick glance at recent profits.

Properly valuing a business can involve weeks of work, sometimes accumulating hundreds of hours. While I can offer a general ballpark estimate based on industry experience—perhaps suggesting a value range between one and a quarter and one and three-quarter million dollars—this would be merely a preliminary figure. A thorough valuation demands a deeper look into the business's financial details and operational nuances. This detailed financial investigation serves multiple purposes. It allows us to prepare comprehensively for the sale and subsequent negotiations. Identifying and explaining any anomalies in the financial records early ensures that all justifications are ready for potential buyers. This groundwork helps smooth the negotiation and due diligence process, providing a solid footing for both buyer and seller.

Even seasoned entrepreneurs might not fully grasp the intricacies of a formal business valuation. It's not just about finding out how much the business is worth but also understanding the potential of what could be left on the table without proper valuation and strategy. Professional guidance can help bridge the gap between personal valuations and market reality, ensuring owners, employees, and customers reap the maximum benefits from any transaction.

## *Preparing Your Business for a Valuation*

While a valuation can technically be done at any point, doing it without preparation often highlights gaps and missed opportunities within your business practices. Many owners don't have a clear understanding of their financials—they rely heavily on their accountant or bookkeeper and, as a result, aren't fully aware of what drives their profits or losses. This lack of insight can be a disadvantage when it's time to sell.

### KNOW YOUR FINANCIALS

To prepare effectively for a valuation, you must know what's happening in your books. Understand what drives profitability in your business and be aware of the areas that could be optimized. You need to identify what assets are to be sold with the business and what you will want to keep (if any). Providing details on any debts the company has, including loans, leases, and financing of any kind, is critical. Having a solid grasp of your accounts payable and receivable is important as well. Understanding your financial statements is essential—not just for your own clarity but also to make your business attractive to potential buyers.

## MINIMIZE RECASTING WORK

Ideally, when preparing for a business valuation, the goal is to minimize the need for what's known as "recasting" work for the last three to five years of business activity. Recasting involves adjusting the financial statements to provide a more accurate picture of the company's financial performance. Often, business owners are what we call "tax efficient," meaning they employ various strategies to minimize their tax burden. This could include writing off extra inventory, claiming personal expenses through the business, or even paying family members for nominal work. While these practices might reduce taxes, they can complicate a valuation process.

## PRESENT A CLEAR FINANCIAL PICTURE

Valuators, me included, prefer financial statements that are straightforward, transparent, and require little adjustment. When your financials reflect a true and accurate picture of the business—without the "extras" like personal expenses or inflated costs—it makes the valuation process smoother. It also helps convince potential buyers and their lenders that the numbers are solid, reducing the risk of them needing forensic audits.

Moreover, a clean set of books can make the quality of earnings report—if you need to go that detailed—much more straightforward. This report often becomes a significant factor in a buyer's lender's decision-making process. Clean, accurate financials help assure buyers and banks that the business is stable, reliable, and worth the investment.

## *More Than Multiples*

One common question I get, not just from sellers but also potential buyers, revolves around the concept of "multiples." Buyers frequently ask, "What multiple did you use to value this business?" The term is thrown around in the media and various financial circles, but the reality is far more complex.

When discussing multiples, specifics matter. Are we considering a multiple of one year's sales? Or perhaps a multiple of EBITDA (Earnings Before Interest, Taxes, Depreciation, and Amortization)? There are also multiples based on the Seller's Discretionary Earnings (SDE) and other financial metrics (SDE equals EBITDA plus one owner's salary and perquisites). Valuations aren't a straightforward application of a single multiple to a single year's financial data. When buyers ask about multiples, they often think it's a quick and easy answer. However, the reality is that multiple factors and various data points are considered to arrive at an accurate valuation.

Part of my role involves educating buyers and sellers about the "lingo" of the industry. Though many people may want to throw terms like "multiple" around just to try and enter the conversation, it's essential for everyone involved to recognize that valuation is more than applying a multiple to a single data point. We must consider the unique aspects of each business and how they translate into market value.

## *The Fear Factor*

A fear among business owners during valuation stems from their long-standing control over their business operations. They've often been the sole decision-makers from day one, and their word has been the final say. Allowing an external party to scrutinize their books and operations can be overwhelming. There's an inherent fear of judgment—what will the valuator say about their management practices? Are there decisions they've made that could be viewed as detrimental to the business's value? This fear of the unknown significantly affects their approach to selling. The possibility of being informed that their business is worth far less than they imagined, or worse, that it's worth nothing, can be a source of significant anxiety. The uncertainty about the outcome of a valuation can be paralyzing. It can lead to hesitation in initiating the process, delaying critical steps toward selling their business.

Addressing this fear involves building trust and providing reassurance. A good business broker approaches these situations with empathy and understanding. Encouraging business owners to see valuation as a beneficial exercise rather than a critique can help alleviate their concerns. Emphasizing that the goal is maximizing the business's value and preparing it for a successful sale can make the process less intimidating. By fostering a supportive environment, owners can gain the confidence to move forward, knowing that the valuation is a tool to help them achieve their ultimate goal of a successful business sale.

In the end, a thorough valuation sets realistic expectations and lays the groundwork for an optimal transition, benefiting both the seller and the buyer. As you embark on this journey, remember that understanding and preparation are your best allies in navigating the complexities of business valuation.

# KEY TAKEAWAYS

➢ Understand that emotional attachment to your business can lead to unrealistic valuations; focus instead on market realities and tangible factors like financial performance and growth potential.

➢ Get a valuation tailored to your specific needs, whether for selling, resolving disputes, or tax purposes and work with someone familiar with your local market to ensure accuracy.

➢ Stay informed on how broader economic factors like interest rates and industry trends, such as consolidation, can impact your business valuation and sale terms.

➢ Properly preparing for a valuation involves knowing your financials and eliminating unnecessary complexities to present a clear, accurate financial picture that appeals to potential buyers.

➢ Valuation involves more than just applying multiples; it requires a comprehensive analysis of various financial metrics and the unique aspects of your business.

# MAXIMIZING YOUR BUSINESS VALUE AFTER TAXES

Several key factors must be considered in maximizing the value of your business. The specifics of each deal can vary greatly depending on the business's nature and the transaction's details. One of the most significant advantages for Canadian business owners is the potential for a substantial tax exemption.

According to the 2025 Lifetime Capital Gains Exemption rules, a portion of the proceeds from the sale of a business, up to $1,250,000, would be tax-free if your business qualifies for the exemption under a share sale. Unfortunately, the Federal Government has changed how this is now calculated, and the rule/exemption amount will continue to change annually for the foreseeable future.

So please consult CRA's website, your accountant, and/or tax lawyer to clarify what this would look like for you.

Most of the business owners I work with in Canada—around 95% or more—definitely prefer a share sale over an asset sale because of this tax benefit. The tax savings alone can be a game-changer for many, significantly impacting their future post-sale.

## *Choosing Between a Share Sale and an Asset Sale*

Business owners' biggest question when selling their business is whether to opt for a share sale or an asset sale. Ultimately, the decision usually comes down to the after-tax dollars the owner will realize once the transaction is completed. Many business owners find the share sale route attractive because of the lifetime capital gains exemption. However, the share sale isn't always the best choice for every situation.

In some cases, an asset sale can be more beneficial. An asset sale involves purchasing specific assets that the company owns and operates, except for the operating shares and some assets the owner may need or want to retain. From a tax perspective, this can sometimes result in better savings, depending on the unique circumstances of the business and the owner's financial goals. The primary goal for most sellers is to maximize the amount of money in their pocket after taxes.

Several myths and misconceptions can cause unnecessary concern, especially when it comes to share sales. One of the most common fears buyers have is the potential for hidden liabilities—what I often refer to as "skeletons in the closet." Buyers sometimes worry that they might be hit with unexpected claims or debts after purchasing a business through a share sale. They fear that creditors or other parties might come forward demanding large sums of money due to issues that arose before they took over. While these concerns are understandable, they are often based on misinformation.

Part of my job is to vet the business thoroughly before the sale. This includes identifying any liabilities, such as ongoing lawsuits or pending claims. If such issues exist, we address them upfront. One common approach is to set aside a portion of the purchase price in a trust or escrow account. This fund covers any liabilities that may arise after the sale. If no issues materialize, the seller receives the funds. If something does come up, the necessary payments are made from this account, ensuring the buyer is protected. And if there's any money left over, then the seller gets the balance.

In addition to escrow accounts, buyers have other protections available in a share sale. Proper insurance coverage can shield both the former owner and the new buyer from liabilities that originated before the sale. The business should have the minimum insurance required by its franchisor, landlord, lender, etc. This includes the proper amount of coverage on any real estate used by the business, any vehicles, heavy machinery, and machines, as well as coverage for the workers. Some businesses have mandated insurance coverages that they need to maintain (remediation, demolition, professional services, etc.).

The final purchase and sale agreements often include covenants, indemnities, representations, and warranties that clearly outline the responsibilities of both parties. These covenants typically state that the seller will be responsible for covering any fees related to issues that occurred on their watch.

Despite initial apprehensions, once buyers understand these protections and the safeguards in place, they generally feel more comfortable proceeding with a share sale. In fact, about 95% of the deals I handle in Canada are completed this way.

## *Balancing Risk and Strategy*

I often see lawyers and buyers continue to harbor fears about what might come back to haunt them after purchasing a business through a share sale. The "what ifs"—like the worry that someone might suddenly demand a large payout due to an old liability—are often overblown. While they can certainly happen, you do need to protect yourself from such events, and there are usually ways to do so without compromising a deal.

The level of risk associated with a share sale versus an asset sale can vary significantly depending on the type of business you're dealing with. For example, the risks are generally lower if you're buying a relatively straightforward business, like a corner convenience store or other retail shop. There is a minimal chance of encountering something severe like life-threatening injuries or lawsuits tied to the business's past activities.

If you're looking at purchasing a business in a high-risk industry—such as a construction or demolition company—there is indeed a higher potential for liabilities that can occur from work completed in the past, which can come back to haunt you. In these cases, buyers' fears may be more justified. However, even in these scenarios, with the right protections and due diligence, these risks can be mitigated.

The larger and more valuable the business, the more due diligence is required. The banks and buyers need to ensure that everything they've been told about the business is accurate. Factoring in a business's level of risk complicates the process further, requiring greater scrutiny.

The insulation business I referred to previously had an outstanding lawsuit against it from a dissatisfied customer. The owner tried to settle the case before closing, but the customer disagreed. So, we ensured that there is enough left in a holdback of funds at closing to account for this, should the business be found at fault and have to pay, and to cover any additional funds should other liabilities present themselves after closing. The key takeaway here is that even though your business might face outstanding liabilities, it may be saleable; we just have to account for them upfront. By the way, the seller of the insulation business won the court case, so he was able to receive all of the money being held back at the end of the holdback period.

At the end of the day, it's all about understanding the actual risks associated with the type of business you're selling. Buyers need to be fully informed and adequately protected, but they must also understand that not all risks are created equally. So, if you own a business that's in the higher risk category, you should be prepared for extra levels of due diligence and be flexible with how the final payment structure will be negotiated, considering the level of risk the buyer could be facing after closing.

### Pivoting from a Share Sale to an Asset Sale

I recently sold a business that illustrates how important it is to stay flexible and be prepared to optimize your sale strategy, even at the last minute. Just this past week, I was initially planning to sell a business as a share sale. We had an accepted offer in place, and everything was moving smoothly toward the end of the due diligence period.

However, during the final stages of due diligence, the seller's accountant discovered that the seller had not withdrawn some excess funds that were sitting in the company's bank account. If the sale proceeded as a share sale, the seller would have faced higher taxes on withdrawing that money afterward. The accountant advised that, in this situation, it would be more tax-efficient to switch to an asset sale. This way, the seller could sell the business assets, pay taxes on that sale, and retain the excess funds within their corporation without the additional tax burden.

Fortunately, we were able to act quickly and modified the final sales documents to change the sale structure from a share sale to an asset sale. This adjustment allowed the business owner to keep the existing corporation while the new buyer acquired all the necessary assets, including the company name, rights, and other elements needed to operate the business successfully moving forward. The outcome was a win-win for both parties—the seller minimized their tax exposure, and the buyer acquired the business assets without any unforeseen complications.

Maximizing your business value involves weighing the benefits and risks of share and asset sales. While the Lifetime Capital Gains Exemption presents a compelling advantage for Canadian business owners opting for a share sale, it is essential to understand the potential risks and have safeguards to protect buyers and sellers. On the other hand, asset sales can sometimes offer strategic tax benefits and reduce exposure to hidden liabilities. Ultimately, the key is flexibility and thorough preparation—understanding your business's unique circumstances, consulting with experts, and being ready to pivot between strategies when necessary. By balancing these considerations and remaining adaptable, business owners can achieve a successful sale that aligns with their financial goals and ensures a smooth transition for both parties involved.

## The Strategic Advantage of a 10-Year Exit Plan

When it comes to selling your business, most owners hear that they should start preparing 3–5 years in advance. And that's sound advice; I used to say the same thing. But the longer I'm in this business, the more I realize that if that's all the time you think you want to put into preparing to sell, that's great, you can still do a fair amount of work in that time. But starting 10 years ahead? That's where the real strategic advantage lies.

A decade-long runway gives you the ability to:

- **Maximize transferable value** – Strengthen systems, build recurring revenue, and reduce owner dependency.
- **Optimize financial performance** – Consistently improve margins and stabilize cash flow, making your business more attractive to premium buyers.
- **Restructure assets tax-efficiently** – Allow time to adjust both company and personal assets to minimize taxes on the eventual sale.
- **Build your leadership team** – Develop strong management capable of running the business without you.
- **Ride out market cycles** – Position yourself to sell when conditions are most favorable, rather than being forced to sell in a downturn.

The earlier you start, the more control you have—not just over the sale price, but over the terms, the buyer pool, and your legacy.

# KEY TAKEAWAYS

> ➢ Deciding between a share sale and an asset sale depends on factors like tax implications, the specific needs of the seller and buyer, and the unique circumstances of the business being sold.

> ➢ The Lifetime Capital Gains Exemption provides a significant tax-saving opportunity for Canadian business owners opting for a share sale, though recent changes have reduced the exemption amount.

> ➢ Concerns about hidden liabilities in share sales are common but can be managed with strategies like escrow accounts, proper insurance, and thorough due diligence to protect both parties.

> ➢ The level of risk in a business sale varies by industry; higher-risk businesses require more extensive scrutiny, while lower-risk businesses may present fewer post-sale complications.

> ➢ Starting to prepare 10 years out and maintaining three to five years of clean books and financials can significantly increase buyer confidence and the potential sale price.

> ➢ Flexibility is crucial in business transactions; being ready to pivot from a share sale to an asset sale, for example, can help optimize financial outcomes and meet the evolving needs of both buyer and seller.

CHAPTER

# WORKING CAPITAL AND CASH FLOWS

One of the hottest topics at every industry conference regarding selling a business is working capital, which often takes up entire workshops. Working capital isn't just a straightforward calculation—it's an element that both sellers and buyers can have very different views on, and those views can significantly affect the outcome of the deal.

Working capital is often a debated and disputed topic among professionals. Even experienced accountants and lawyers can have varying interpretations of what should be included in working capital when selling a business. The interpretation can depend on the nature of the business. For example, a manufacturing company might have a different working capital requirement than a service-based company, and this difference can lead to discrepancies.

For smaller, Main Street businesses (that sell for $3,000,000 or less), the basic formula for calculating working capital is:

**Working Capital = Current Assets - Current Liabilities**

However, when dealing with larger businesses, $5,000,000 to $50,000,000 and up, this formula becomes much more complicated. For larger businesses with complex structures, consider the following ratios as well.

> **Days Sales Outstanding (DSO):** Accounts Receivable + (Sales / Days in period)

> **Days Inventory Outstanding (DIO):** Inventory / (Cost of Goods Sold "Inventory" / Days in period)

> **Days Payable Outstanding (DPO):** Accounts Payable "Suppliers" / (Product Purchases / Days in period)

In addition to these ratios, there are two types of working capital: permanent and temporary. Then there are at least 16 working capital determinants that help to break down the different aspects of it, to decide what should be included in the sale. I'm not going to focus on all those details, as I want this book to be more of a handbook than a textbook.

Sellers typically want to leave as little working capital as possible in a deal and take as much cash out as possible. On the other hand, buyers often prefer to have a little more working capital left in the business. This extra cushion can sustain them longer after the deal closes. A buyer stepping into a business needs to be assured that they won't have to inject additional capital immediately after the purchase to keep the business running. For instance, they don't want to invest an extra $100,000 to $500,000 to cover the basics like inventory, materials, and payroll while waiting for revenue streams to stabilize. They want to step into a business that is ready to go, with sufficient working capital to support ongoing operations without additional cash outlays. Therefore, understanding what constitutes an appropriate amount of working capital and negotiating it is crucial for both buyers and sellers.

The calculation becomes intricate when it comes to complex businesses, such as a construction company earning $20 million-a-year in revenue. These companies might have multiple layers of inventory—jobs nearing completion, jobs just getting started, and jobs fully underway—all requiring a certain level of working capital. Such inventory will often be included in the Work-in-Progress (WIP) -this is a construction, service-based business-related term. Work-in-Process (WIP) is used in the manufacturing industry. Beyond inventory, there needs to be enough cash to cover payroll and ongoing bills, especially considering that some businesses don't see payments from their customers for 60, 90, or even 180 days after a job is completed.

Working capital involves more than just cash and inventory. If a limited amount of money is available on hand, it could include accounts receivable. Additionally, debt obligations may be tied to working capital, accounts payable as owed for current inventory and wages, and outstanding customer deposits or gift cards issued that need to be honored. All of these elements need to be accounted for when preparing the business for sale. This preparation often involves some hard truths. I always strive to educate business owners early on in the process that if you want to sell your business for a certain price, you need to account for and ensure you're leaving enough working capital to maintain its current operations.

## *Inventory Practices: The Hidden Problem*

One of the biggest misconceptions about working capital revolves around inventory practices. For tax purposes, many business owners might engage in "writing off" inventory, thereby reducing the amount of inventory on their books to decrease their tax liabilities at the end of the year. While this might seem like a smart move at tax time, it can create complications when selling the business.

Imagine a scenario where a business has a warehouse full of perfectly good, sellable inventory that isn't reflected on their books. When it comes time to sell, the owner might think, "Great, I've got all this extra inventory to sweeten the deal." However, buyers don't see it that way. They ask, "Why should I take on excess inventory that isn't reflected in your financials? Why should I be burdened with it if you couldn't sell it?" Even if a buyer is willing to take on the excess inventory, how will it be paid for? Will you add the value to any seller financing? Would you be willing to have the buyer take it on consignment and get paid when / if it sells? Will the bank be willing to finance it? Or will the buyer have to come up with extra cash at closing?

What if some of the above inventory is a couple of years old, or older? I've seen inventory hidden away in basements or mezzanines that are literally covered in dust. Just how salable is that inventory? Often, this would be considered obsolete inventory, and the buyer wants nothing to do with it.

The lesson here is simple: clean up your inventory practices early.

It may take a couple of years to get things in order, but ensuring your inventory is accurately reflected in your financials will prevent headaches when it comes time to sell. Buyers want to see a well-organized operation where inventory practices make sense.

## *Are You Being the Bank?*

Another misconception involves accounts receivable. Some business owners are slow in collecting their invoices, essentially acting as a bank for their customers. While this may keep customers happy, it significantly impacts your cash flow. When buyers evaluate your business, they consider cash flow to be a significant factor. If they see delayed collections, they might wonder if they are walking into a cash flow nightmare.

To avoid this, it's wise to start collecting payments promptly, well before you decide to sell. If your business has gotten used to lenient payment terms with clients, you'll need a couple of years to adjust your collection methods. Buyers want a business where the cash is coming in consistently and promptly, allowing them to operate comfortably without immediate cash flow concerns.

These misconceptions highlight a broader point—you don't prepare your business for sale overnight. It takes time, sometimes years, to fine-tune your practices to align with what buyers are looking for. Adjusting your inventory methods, cleaning up accounts receivable (and your accounts payable), and ensuring your financials are in order can make your business more appealing and significantly increase the chances of a smooth sale.

While there isn't a one-size-fits-all number to quantify this relationship, the principle is that a well-documented, properly managed, and well-cash-flowed business will always attract more serious buyers who are willing to pay a premium for a transparent, well-run operation.

## *Peaks and Valleys*

One final point I'd like to emphasize is the complexity of working capital and how imperative it is to understand when selling a business. As discussed previously, when a business grows and diversifies, its working capital requirements become more complex. But what about when cash flows fluctuate seasonally?

For this reason, it's essential to work with professionals who understand the intricacies involved and can identify what needs to be considered right from the start. That's why, when I step in to help, I always request monthly financials for at least the last two years of operations. This allows me to see the ebbs and flows of cash flow, inventory levels, accounts payable, and receivables.

Timing the sale of a business also plays a role in working capital discussions. If a business is being sold during its peak season—a landscaping business that does well in the spring—there might be a lot of excess inventory and payables on the books that need to be accounted for in the sale price. Conversely, if the sale occurs during a slower period (such as winter), the inventory would be nearly depleted. Instead of higher payables, there would likely be a higher accounts receivable balance, requiring adjustments to reflect the working capital requirement.

Seasonality and timing are particularly important for asset-intensive or current liability-heavy businesses. Knowing when to sell and how the timing affects the numbers can make a big difference in how the deal is structured and negotiated.

Remember, this process doesn't happen overnight. It takes time, sometimes years, to fine-tune these aspects and present a business ready to sell at its full potential. By understanding these factors and planning strategically, you can maximize the value of your business and ensure a smoother, more successful sale that benefits both you and the future owner.

## KEY TAKEAWAYS

➤ Working capital is a complex and often debated topic in business sales. It requires clear definitions and negotiation to meet both buyers' and sellers' needs.

➤ Misconceptions about inventory practices and accounts receivable can create complications; it is essential to prepare well in advance with clean, transparent financials.

➤ Timing the sale and understanding seasonality's impact on working capital is crucial for structuring a fair and successful deal.

CHAPTER

# TAXES

Let's be candid for a minute here. Many business owners are as "tax efficient" as possible when it comes to reporting their income and expenses to the government for tax purposes. And frankly, I understand this mentality, I really do. But this is the wrong approach when it comes time to sell your business.

While lowering tax liabilities by not claiming certain items accurately may seem appealing in the short term, this strategy can backfire when it's time to sell. Saving a few thousand dollars on taxes in the short term could cost you much more in the long run. If you conduct your business operations and tax filings properly, in line with standard business practices, you stand to gain far more when you sell the business. For instance, suppose you paid $15,000 in taxes by accurately reporting your inventory and other financial details. By doing so, you could increase the value of your business by much more than that tax expense when it's time to sell.

When buyers look at a potential acquisition, they scrutinize everything, especially tax records. If they notice discrepancies or creative accounting practices that skew the business's actual financial health, they might view it as a red flag. This could result in reduced offers or, worse, no offers at all. Proper tax practices assure buyers that the business is not hiding any unpleasant surprises.

If a business can maintain clean books, paying taxes appropriately and accurately reflecting its true financial position for three to five years leading up to the sale, it provides a significant advantage. Buyers—and, importantly, the banks funding these buyers—will have far more faith in the numbers presented. A buyer who sees consistent, well-maintained books over several years is more likely to view the business as a solid investment. The potential return on investment from maintaining clean financials far outweighs any costs associated with proper tax payments or hiring professional accountants to ensure everything is in order.

As tempting as it may be, my best advice regarding working capital is to avoid shortcuts, like manipulating inventory or delaying tax payments. It might offer short-term relief, but it can undermine the true value of your business. Instead, investing in clean books, maintaining appropriate working capital, managing work-in-progress, and managing your accounts receivable and payable efficiently will position your business as a well-run, reliable investment, attracting serious buyers who are willing to pay a premium for confidence and stability.

Short-term tax savings tactics can lead to reduced business value; proper tax practices enhance appeal to buyers and support higher sale prices.

## Lifetime Capital Gains Exemption (LTCGE)

Here we will build upon the previous points made about the LTCGE in Chapter Three (Choosing Between a Share Sale and an Asset Sale). This is an important consideration for many entrepreneurs that I work with, understandably so. If you could sell your business and either not pay any taxes or have the amount of taxes you do pay reduced, why wouldn't you take advantage of that?

At the time this book is published, the Lifetime Capital Gains Exemption in Canada stands at CAD $1,250,000 per shareholder, for qualified small business shares and farm/fishing assets. Though not yet enacted into law, the government has explicitly confirmed its intent to uphold this increased limit. So, if a solopreneur were to sell their business for $1,250,000, then they wouldn't have to pay taxes on that amount. Similarly, if there were two shareholders, they could sell their business for $2,500,000, and each would receive the same benefit. And so on. Naturally, it's not always that simple, so please consult your professional tax accountant and/or lawyer to clarify how this rule could be applied to your transition.

## Excess Assets

Switching gears and going back to an asset sale structure for a moment. Sometimes, as part of a tax strategy, business owners have excess assets on their company balance sheet. This could be cash or investments (e.g., stocks, bonds, insurance policies). I've also seen personal cars, boats, planes, houses, cottages, and so on, in the company's books. If these assets are not being used or are not required for regular operations, they should be removed from the company's balance sheet before sale. This process often takes several years to be done as tax-efficiently as possible.

Also, if you're considering an asset sale, you should be aware of something called Recapture Tax. This is something that CRA will charge against the proceeds of your sale, if applicable. Recapture Tax is triggered when you sell your assets for more than their net book value (the value declared on your most recent balance sheet). For example, say that your vehicles have been fully depreciated and their value on the current balance sheet is $0. But on closing, the accountants assign $250,000 of the sale price to the vehicles you've just sold. That means that CRA will charge you the Recapture Tax based on the $250,000. What exactly that tax rate will be depends on your specific circumstances at closing. That's where I always defer to the accountants and/or tax lawyers about this part of the deal structure. Hence, the importance of proper tax planning before going to market, so you understand the implications of an asset and a share sale.

Please be advised that in each of these situations, the rules change regularly. As such, I recommend that you speak with a knowledgeable tax accountant and/or lawyer on how to navigate any of the above circumstances best.

## KEY TAKEAWAYS

➤ Reducing your tax bill in the short term by underreporting income or inflating expenses might save you now, but it can dramatically lower your business's value when it's time to sell.

➤ Clean, accurate financials—maintained over several years—build trust with buyers and lenders, making your business more appealing and valuable.

➤ Avoid manipulating inventory, delaying tax payments, or cutting corners with working capital; serious buyers pay premiums for transparency and reliability.

➤ The Lifetime Capital Gains Exemption can significantly reduce or eliminate taxes on the sale of a business in Canada—if you plan properly.

➤ Excess personal or non-operational assets on the balance sheet should be removed well before selling; work with a qualified tax professional to do this efficiently.

# LAWYERS, LIABILITIES, AND LEGAL SAFEGUARDS

The legal aspects of a business sale touch every single deal. There really is no exception. Legal considerations show up in different ways, at different stages, and often when business owners least expect them.

There is an old saying that "you do not know what you do not know." In the legal world of selling a business, that saying can come back to hurt you in a very real way. Many sellers do not understand the ramifications if they do not protect themselves. By the time they realize something has been missed, it is often too late or costly to fix. One of the most important decisions you will make at this stage is choosing the right lawyer who truly understands business transactions.

I can share a story that, unfortunately, illustrates what happens when the wrong lawyer is selected. About four or five years ago, I was involved in a transaction where someone was buying a garage. The buyer was referred to a lawyer by a friend. It was a special relationship between the one who made the referral and the buyer, and on the surface, everything seemed fine. I did my initial research on the lawyer, and their website said they handled this kind of transaction before. Based on that, it appeared as though they should have been qualified.

As we moved through the process, everything seemed okay at first. But when we got right down to closing, it became evident that the buyer's lawyer had no idea how to draft the documents required to close the deal.

At that point, the seller's lawyer stepped in and made it very clear that this was not their responsibility. They were not there to teach another lawyer how to do their job. If they did, they would have to bill their own client more. Naturally, the sellers were getting upset because they did not want to pay any more in legal fees than necessary.

I strongly suggested to the buyer that they should fire their lawyer and bring in someone with actual experience. But because of the relationship tied to the referral, the buyer felt that they could not do that without creating problems outside of the sale that they did not want to deal with.

So we had to get creative.

The sellers eventually agreed that their lawyer would draft the documents that the buyer's lawyer should have been doing and essentially teach them how to complete the work. The buyer then reimbursed the seller for those additional legal fees.

This was a very unique situation. Normally, the recommendation would have been straightforward. Fire the lawyer and replace them with someone who knows how to do these deals. I typically refer the buyer or seller to a few qualified lawyers whom I know can get transactions like this done.

The lesson here is that business sale transactions are specialized. They are a niche area of law. If a lawyer does not have direct experience with these types of deals, they need to have access to someone within their firm who does. They need someone they can lean on and who can guide them through the process. Without that experience, mistakes happen, costs increase, and deals are put at risk.

## Understanding What You Are Signing

There are many different documents used at the early stages of negotiating a deal. You will hear terms like Expressions of Interest (EoIs), Indications of Interest (IoIs), Notices of Interest (NoIs), and Letters of Intent (LoIs), which are typically drafted by the buyer's lawyer. Despite the different names, these documents are essentially the same thing. They usually cover the same types of terms and serve the same purpose. They are the initial starting point for negotiations.

I prefer a different approach: using an Offer to Purchase (OtP) that I would draft. An offer to purchase is very similar to those other documents, but it goes into much more detail. In addition to having our standard representations and warranties, it covers the key terms we want agreed to upfront and serves as the foundation for the final legal documents. These conditions and terms can include defining the structure of the deal (e.g. what is paid at closing, how much will be seller finance and at what terms), how to manage employees, insurances, intellectual property, real estate, vehicles, websites, what is included and not included in the deal (from a balance sheet perspective), who is responsible to pay for what, defining timelines for completing various conditions, and much more. The more clearly these major terms are defined and agreed upon in the early stages, the less likely it is that a sale will fall apart later. Deals often die later, after the accountants and lawyers have started their hourly billing, because too many assumptions were made early and never documented.

Another critical point is understanding whether the document you are signing is binding, non-binding, or partially binding. Quite often, only certain clauses within these documents are binding, while the rest are not. The document itself should specify which parts are binding and which are not.

You need to pay close attention to this. No matter what the document is called, you must understand what obligations you are agreeing to and where you could be exposed. Signing something without fully understanding the legal implications can put you in a position you never intended to be in. Legal documents shape the deal, protect your interests, and help ensure that what you think you are agreeing to is what actually happens.

## How Bank Loans, VTBs, and Earnouts Work Together in the Real World

Earnouts are one of the most effective tools for getting a deal done. When structured properly, they can allow the seller to make more money after closing than was initially agreed upon, while also protecting the buyer if the business does not perform as hoped.

We all know things can happen. Industries change. Markets shift. Sometimes you have very strong confidence that certain contracts or revenue streams will continue because they have historically.

You may even have reassurances from clients that the deals will go through. Then something entirely outside of anyone's control happens. Policy changes. Economies shift. Cross-border rules change. Suddenly, the business is not performing as everyone expected. An earnout helps address that uncertainty.

If the business earns less than a specific target, the buyer is not obligated to pay more than what is justified by performance. From the buyer's perspective, that protection is critical. From the seller's perspective, the upside is attractive: if the business performs well, they can earn more than the original purchase price. That combination often helps save deals that might otherwise stall or fall apart.

That said, earnouts come with important caveats. You need to be very clear on what the earnout benchmark is based on. Is it sales revenue? Gross revenue? Net profit? Each of those carries different risks. Typically, you want the benchmark set as close as possible to the top line of the profit and loss statement. Sales, net sales, or gross sales are usually safer. The further down the income statement you go, the more room there can be for numbers to be influenced in ways that affect how much the buyer ultimately has to pay you. That is something sellers absolutely need to be cognizant of.

## THE ROLE BANKS PLAY IN STRUCTURING THE DEAL

In most transactions, banks will play a role. In the eleven years I have been doing this, I have only had about four or five deals where the seller did not have to hold any money at all on the sale of their business.

When banks are involved, they often dictate the terms of the sale. That includes how financing is repaid to the seller, the maximum interest rate that can be charged, and whether or not principal payments can begin immediately. In many cases, especially with institutions like the Business Development Bank of Canada (BDC), there are safeguards built in to protect the business's future.

Quite often, for the first 2 to 5 years after closing, the seller may only be paid interest, not principal. Principal repayments only begin if the business performance meets specific benchmarks. If the business is doing well enough after the first, the bank may allow principal payments to start earlier. If not, interest-only payments continue.

There are also considerations regarding who holds the first position against the business's assets in case of a default on the loan payments. In most cases, the bank will be in first position. Sellers and everyone else come after that. Banks will always protect their interests first. That is the reality of how these deals work.

The good news is this. Banks are highly risk-averse, so if a bank is willing to lend several million dollars to a buyer to purchase your business, that should give you some confidence as well. Banks make their money by betting on people they believe can pay them back. If they have vetted the buyer thoroughly and are confident enough to lend, that validation matters. It's not a guarantee, but it should be a good indicator.

## Vendor Take-Backs and First Position Demands

A Vendor Take-Back (VTB), or seller note, is the portion of the purchase price the seller finances to help make the deal happen. For example, if a business sells for five million dollars, the buyer may put in one million, the bank may lend three million, and the seller may hold one million. That last one million is the vendor take-back.

Many sellers want to be in the first position and are uncomfortable being behind the bank. That is understandable. However, when the bank provides the majority of the capital, it is almost always in the driver's seat. Their position is straightforward: *This is how we are willing to lend the money. If you do not like the terms, you do not have to take it, but the transaction will not happen without our money.*

Sometimes there is wiggle room. If the buyer can put in more of their own capital, or if the seller is willing to hold more financing to reduce the bank's exposure, negotiations can shift the bank's terms slightly. But when the bank is required to make the deal happen, they will dictate the structure. Even then, it is not always as scary as it seems. Again, if the bank has completed its due diligence and believes the buyer is qualified, that should provide the seller with some reassurance.

Yes, there are horror stories out there. You can find them quickly online. I have heard them from business owners in my own area as well. But I have never personally been involved in a sale where a seller was not paid what they were owed.

## Why Insurance Is a Two-Way Street for Buyers and Sellers

Most people only think about insurance from one angle: putting insurance on the buyer to protect the seller's vendor financing if something happens after closing.

Using a simple example: if a business sells for $5 million and the seller is holding $1 million in financing, the seller wants that $1 million protected. If the buyer is relocating from somewhere else in the country or even from another part of the world, and something occurs during or after closing that leaves them unable to physically or mentally operate the business, the seller should not lose the money they are contractually owed. That is why sellers want insurance in place, just like banks do, to protect their financing.

But insurance is not just about protecting the seller.

I had a deal just a year or two ago where the buyer purchased a business from someone who was literally the name and the face of the company. The company operated under that individual's personal name. The buyer purchased the business with the expectation that the seller would continue to work, refer business, and help with the transition.

Later that summer, the seller was in an accident and passed away.

Suddenly, the buyer owned a business where the primary driver of revenue, the person whose reputation built the company, was gone. The business was no longer worth anywhere near what it had been at the time of purchase.

That is why I strongly recommend insurance not just for buyers, but also for key people. That can include sellers who remain on post-closing, key managers, CFOs, or anyone else crucial to the ongoing success of the business. If something happens to them, having the right insurance in place can help mitigate both the financial and operational impact. Insurance is not one-sided. When done correctly, it protects all parties. Specifying the requirement for these protections in the Offer to Purchase sets the expectations early on that the interest of both parties is being looked after.

## Issues That Catch Sellers Off Guard

Liabilities have a way of surfacing at the worst possible time if they are not disclosed early. I once worked on a sale involving an insulation business where a customer claimed the work was done improperly and caused damage to their home. The business owner disagreed. The issue went back and forth, and eventually the customer decided to sue.

As is often the case, the court system moved very slowly. The dispute dragged on for years. They attempted mediation, and the mediator sided with the business owner. The customer was unhappy with that result, ignored the mediation outcome, and pursued the case in court.

When I became involved, we made sure that the situation was fully disclosed. It was clearly outlined in the marketing materials and discussed openly during negotiations and diligence. As such, the buyer's lawyer was fully aware of the ongoing court case.

At closing, a portion of the purchase price was held back to protect against any outcome from that lawsuit or any other unknown liabilities, which is standard practice with situations like this.

About six to eight months after the deal closed, the court case was finally resolved, and the seller was completely absolved of any wrongdoing. As a result, the seller received all of the money that had been held back.

As long as we know about these issues, they can usually be handled appropriately. If you are dealing with a potential two-million-dollar lawsuit on a two-hundred-and-fifty-thousand-dollar business, that is going to be very difficult to manage. But if the risk is proportional and manageable, there are ways to structure the sale to account for it.

That is why I need to know about everything. Lines of credit, capital leases, mortgages, pending (legal) disputes, and any other liabilities. When all of that information is presented at the beginning, deals have a tendency to move much more smoothly.

## ENVIRONMENTAL AND SAFETY SURPRISES

Environmental concerns are another area that can derail a sale if they are not addressed properly. For any commercial property sale, banks require at least a phase one environmental report. It is mandatory. A phase one is a historical review of the property to determine whether there is a potential for contamination, either from past use of the property or from neighboring properties where contamination could have migrated.

Today, phase one reports typically cost between $3,500 and $5,000, depending on the nature of the property. I often recommend that the buyer and seller split the cost. That way, if the deal does not proceed with that buyer, the seller still has a copy of the report that can be used for future negotiations.

If a phase one identifies potential concerns, a phase two may be required. That could involve soil and/or water sampling and more detailed testing. Phase twos can become significantly more expensive, depending on what is needed. This can get a little more costly; you could end up paying $15,000, depending on the nature of the work.

If contamination is confirmed, a phase three is then required. That is where remediation takes place. At that point, the process becomes much more complex, and more often than not, the responsibility falls on the seller. Buyers are generally reluctant to pay for extensive testing or cleanup on a property they do not yet own, especially considering that they had nothing to do with whatever caused the contamination in the first place.

The upside is that once a phase three is completed and remediation is successful, the issue is essentially resolved. That report stays with the property. As long as nothing changes, future sales typically do not require further environmental testing, and the property can change hands without ongoing concerns, provided no further contamination occurs.

These issues can feel overwhelming, but when they are identified early, they do not have to kill a deal. Like everything else in this process, transparency and preparation make all the difference.

## *Non-Compete and Non-Solicit Agreements*

Non-compete and non-solicit agreements can feel tricky for sellers, but there is usually no way around them. And when you look at it from the buyer's perspective, they make complete sense.

If you were buying a business for five million dollars by putting one million of your own money and effectively paying four million more over time, you would want to know that the person you purchased the business from, and any of their key employees or relatives, is not going to set up shop across town and start competing with you.

Imagine that you are still paying the seller while they are competing against you. They bring over their contacts, recruit your staff, and negotiate better supplier terms because they are starting fresh and are using their influence and history to their advantage. Suddenly, they have a competitive advantage. That situation would not sit well with anyone. That is exactly what buyers are trying to protect themselves from. Lawyers on both sides will always insist on this type of protection.

How restrictive these agreements are depends on the nature of the business. Courts generally recognize that everyone has the right to earn a living. They are not going to prevent someone from earning an income altogether. What they will enforce is preventing direct competition with the business sold, so the seller is not acting in bad faith in the transaction.

Typically, the length of non-compete and non-solicit agreements aligns with the financing terms. If the loans run for five years, the restrictions often last at least that long. Sometimes they are longer to add extra protection.

If a seller truly plans to retire and has no intention of returning to the industry, these terms are rarely a sticking point.When sellers resist signing a non-compete, it makes buyers (and me) nervous. Buyers start questioning the seller's intentions after the sale. If the seller does not plan to compete, why would they object?

These agreements are a critical part of protecting the integrity of the deal and reflect the trust and good faith built during the process. The general terms of these agreements should also be agreed on in the Offer to Purchase. This gives the lawyers a starting point when drafting and negotiating these aspects of the closing documents.

## Employment Agreements After Closing

Employment agreements play a major role in what happens after closing. When sellers stay involved for a period of time, there are significant benefits. The biggest one is guidance. A seller who has run a business for twenty or thirty years has seen situations that a new owner may be experiencing for the first time. Being available to guide the new owner through those early challenges helps prevent costly mistakes and keeps operations steady. That stability protects revenue and profitability. It also protects everyone's financial interests, including the bank and the seller if there is vendor financing in place.

In many deals, sellers stay on for anywhere from six months to a couple of years. Sometimes they are on payroll. Other times, they work as independent contractors. It is important to discuss this with both your lawyer and your accountant. The structure of that arrangement has tax implications, especially if you are receiving employment income in addition to vendor financing or other payments after closing. You want that set up as tax-efficiently as possible.

Employment agreements are not just for sellers. They are equally important for key employees.

If there is a key manager, engineer, or specialist whose presence directly affects the business's value, that person needs to be secured. If they were not already on a solid employment contract before closing, this is the time to put one in place. These agreements should clarify benefits, compensation, incentives, raises, and vacation entitlements.

They also define what happens if employment ends. Termination and severance provisions need to be clearly outlined. Without that clarity, it falls to the courts to decide what someone is entitled to, and that creates uncertainty for new owners.

Unionized employees add another layer. Some buyers are comfortable with unions and understand how to work within those structures. Others want nothing to do with unionized workforces. If your employees are unionized, the terms of those agreements must be understood upfront.

Finally, timing matters. There is a right time and a wrong time to tell employees about a sale. Some buyers want to meet key employees early. Others prefer to wait. In some cases, certain employees need to be brought in sooner because they are essential to providing information for due diligence.

All of these details need to be addressed as part of the process.

When employment agreements, communication timing, and expectations are correctly handled, they set the tone for employee loyalty, retention, and a smoother transition after closing.

Having timelines and a general process for dealing with employees agreed upon when negotiating the Offer to Purchase removes any ambiguity, incorrect assumptions for both parties, and makes that part of the diligence and closing process run smoothly.

## Protect Yourself Without Breaking the Deal

The tricky part about selling a business is finding the balance between protection and progress. Your lawyer's job is to protect you and your family during the closing documentation. That part is non-negotiable. Where things can go sideways is when that protection turns into obstruction.

Some lawyers take pride in being deal killers. That is just their personality and the reputation they want to have. Then some lawyers are deal makers. They understand that every transaction has risk, and their job is to identify it, explain it to you in a way that you will clearly understand it, and help mitigate as much of it as possible without blowing up the deal. Those are the lawyers you want on your side.

I often compare negotiations to a teeter-totter. If one lawyer pushes all the risk onto the other side, the balance tips too far in their favour. If the other lawyer then pushes back, now the balance swings too far the other way. If that keeps happening, the teeter-totter eventually breaks, and the deal dies. A successful transaction requires both sides to accept that some level of risk exists and that they can share it and still get the deal closed.

Another issue I see too often is lawyers trying to renegotiate business terms that have already been agreed to in the offer to purchase or letter of intent. Those terms are usually the result of months of work and careful negotiation. When a lawyer comes in late in the process and starts reopening those discussions, it creates distrust and frustration. Sellers start wondering what else will change, buyers do the same, and deals fall apart because of it.

That does not mean lawyers should not raise concerns. If something was missed or a risk was not properly considered, it absolutely needs to be addressed. But reopening agreed-upon terms to renegotiate or to try to make themselves "look good" rarely ends well. Sometimes issues arise simply because a clause was left in from a previous template that was never meant to apply to your particular sale. Catching those things early can save a lot of unnecessary tension. That is why I strongly recommend that your lawyer share draft documents with your business broker, preferably before they are sent to opposing counsel, so we can remain involved in the document drafting to help prevent misunderstandings.

When choosing a lawyer, ask real questions. How many transactions have they worked on? More importantly, how many actually closed? Experience matters, but successfully completed deals matter more.

The reality is that entire law courses are dedicated to business and real estate transactions. We cannot cover every nuance here. The purpose of this chapter is to give you a window into why things are done the way they are and why I ask for the information I do. Every question, every document request, and every disclosure plays a role in protecting you while also helping ensure a smooth transition to the next owner. My goal throughout this process is simple. Protect your interests, identify and manage risk, and keep the deal moving forward in a way that makes sense for everyone.

When the right professionals work together, and the right balance is maintained, legal safeguards do not have to slow things down. They become what they are meant to be: a foundation for a successful sale and a clean transition into the next phase of your life.

## KEY TAKEAWAYS

➢ Choose a lawyer who understands business transactions and knows how to get deals closed, not someone learning on your dime or trying to make a name by killing deals.

➢ Know exactly what you are signing and which parts of any document are binding, because incorrect assumptions made early are often what derail deals late in the process.

➢ Earnouts, bank financing, and vendor take-backs can work well together when they are structured clearly, and benchmarks are set in a way that protects both sides.

➢ Full disclosure of liabilities, environmental issues, and risks upfront allows deals to be appropriately structured, rather than falling apart under pressure later.

➢ The right balance between legal protection and forward momentum keeps lawyers focused on safeguarding the deal without breaking it.

➢ Make sure to address as many key deal terms as possible in the Offer to Purchase or other initial agreements to avoid potentially costly legal bills and/or misunderstandings that will kill your deal.

# MARKETING YOUR BUSINESS

Marketing is essential for any business endeavor. If you don't market your product or business strategically, your sales will suffer. But when it comes to selling your business, the approach to marketing takes on a unique twist. Unlike traditional marketing, where word-of-mouth promotion might work wonders, the last thing you want is to let it slip that your business is for sale. Confidential marketing is required to get your message out without compromising the value of your business or unsettling employees, clients, and/or suppliers. This is not an easy thing to do, especially if the business is located in a smaller geographic market, trying to write an ad for your business that will not identify it can be very difficult.

Here's where things get a bit tricky: Do you have the expertise to handle this kind of marketing on your own? In addition to writing the ad that the public will see, creating and distributing marketing materials that capture the right details about your business is a huge task. If they look thrown together or lack professionalism (or you forget to use spell check), buyers may question the value and seriousness of your offering. Imagine receiving a basic, hastily prepared summary with a few pages of key attributes and financials. If it doesn't appear professional, why would you waste your time in exploring it further? Professionally designed documents can make a world of difference, distinguishing your business from the competition and enhancing its appeal.

Effective marketing also demands an understanding of prospective buyers' mindsets. What makes your business a worthwhile investment, especially when you compare it against all of the other businesses that are for sale? Make no mistake, buyers are looking at more than one business at a time, so you need to find a way to make your business stand out above the others. What aspects do they need to know to make an informed decision? If you don't have insight into what buyers are looking for, you're already at a disadvantage.

The marketing strategy must be as unique as the business itself. Each industry—and each individual business—requires a tailored approach. Interested buyers will need specific information to make informed decisions, but you must control what is shared and when. Potential buyers will want to know the following:

- → **Financials:** Financial data, trends, and a detailed analysis.
- → **History and Background:** A concise business history outlining significant milestones and challenges overcome.

→ **Future Potential:** Insights into how the business is positioned for future growth.

→ **Employee Structure:** A breakdown of your team and key roles.

→ **Assets and Liabilities:** Details about assets, any outstanding debt, and excluded items from the sale.

These are just the basics; depending on your business, the amount of information can be extensive. Take, for instance, a marina business I'm currently marketing. I've assembled five separate documents for this transaction, plus a video interview with the business owner. The documents cover everything from in-depth financial analyses to property evaluations and responses to questions from prospective buyers.

A marketing tool I've embraced—and which is still gaining traction here in Canada—is the use of video interviews. While many brokers in the U.S. and other countries have already incorporated video into their process, it's just starting to catch on here. These video interviews, typically lasting between an hour to an hour and a half, allow buyers to get an in-depth, firsthand view of the business directly from the owner's (your) mouth. These videos offer transparency and allow prospective buyers to build trust with the owner as they can often relate to them, and I use text from the interview to enhance the written materials, creating a more cohesive narrative.

Remember that not every inquiry warrants full access to your business's sensitive details. You'll need a structured process to manage information flow, ensuring that only qualified buyers gain access to critical data at the right time. Many brokers use secure tools and software to handle these disclosures, each adopting a slightly different way to achieve similar results.

One of the biggest mistakes business owners make when marketing their own businesses is overexposing their information. For example, when someone shows interest in your business and asks for financials, the excitement might drive you to pull a quick non-disclosure agreement (NDA) off the internet, get it signed, and then send over detailed financials. But financials should be one of the last pieces of information you share, not the first. Numbers are important, but they don't tell the whole story. Rather than handing over the numbers right away, focus on introducing the prospective buyer to the full scope of your business. Share insights into the business's operations, team, and culture first, and keep a tight handle on when financial data gets shared.

## *Enhancing Your Company's Appeal Through Branding and Marketing*

Improving your company's branding and marketing isn't an overnight fix, but there are ways to start elevating your business's appeal to potential buyers.

### SPRUCING UP THE PHYSICAL SPACE

Begin with the physical environment. Whether you own or lease your business space, a well-presented location can make a lasting impression. As a business owner, you see your space daily and may overlook areas that could use a refresh. Bringing in an outsider—someone unfamiliar with the business—can offer a fresh perspective. Small changes, like applying a fresh coat of paint to the entranceway, waiting and/or board rooms, or power washing the workshop, can make a significant difference. Take the time to tackle those cobwebs in the corner or the old fluorescent tube lighting that hasn't been changed since the '80s. It doesn't need to be staged like a home for sale, but a tidy, clean, and well-maintained environment signals to buyers that the business is cared for and ready for new ownership.

## Strengthening Your Online Presence

For most businesses today, your online presence is as important as your physical location. Potential buyers are likely to check your website, social media, and online reviews. Start by managing your reviews—address any negative feedback and showcase positive testimonials. If your most recent testimonial is two or more years old, reach out to recent clients to gather updated feedback. Buyers want to see that your business has been active and positively reviewed in the current market, not just in the past.

Ensure that your website and social media profiles reflect your brand's current activities, products, or services. Outdated content, such as a last blog post from five years ago, can give an impression of stagnation. Updating and keeping these areas current shows buyers that the business has maintained its reputation and engagement over time. Don't forget to use spell and grammar checking as well for your online presence!

## *Measuring the Success of Your Marketing Efforts*

Success is ultimately defined by whether or not you achieve the sale, but along the way, there are several indicators that can help you assess and refine your efforts. Consider the level of positive responses your marketing generates. For instance, if you've employed digital outreach or targeted ads, track the number of serious inquiries. If your campaign isn't yielding responses, it may be time to revisit and adjust your messaging. This process might involve changing the way you present key information or making your marketing materials more appealing to the target audience.

A high volume of inquiries isn't enough if those interested lack the qualifications to make a purchase. For example, if you're marketing a business with a $1 million price tag but receiving interest from individuals with much lower budgets, it's a sign that your messaging might need to be more targeted. Adjusting the ad to filter for more qualified buyers can help you focus on those who have both the financial resources and the interest to proceed with the acquisition.

In my experience, we miss the mark when our ad descriptions are too general. If the message is too broad, it can attract people who aren't the right fit. For example, we might initially get a high volume of responses, but after a quick call, many potential buyers lose interest because the business isn't what they're actually seeking. This means reworking the language to clarify key attributes, such as the industry, size, and opportunity, without revealing identifying details. A well-targeted description can prevent unqualified buyer candidates, saving time and bringing us closer to securing the right buyer.

Marketing your business for sale requires a careful balance of confidentiality, strategy, and presentation. From identifying what information to share and when to managing inquiries and enhancing your brand, every step impacts how buyers view your business and their level of trust in what you say. Investing the time and resources into doing it right will pay off when buyers easily see why your business is worth their investment.

# KEY TAKEAWAYS

➢ Confidentiality in marketing protects the business while attracting qualified buyers, requiring a tailored, professional approach to creating and sharing materials.

➢ Marketing materials should be well-designed and convey professionalism, as sloppy or incomplete information may turn off serious buyers.

➢ Understanding buyer's perspectives and focusing on financials, history, growth potential, and team structure paints a comprehensive picture.

➢ Preparing your physical and online presence shows buyers the business is cared for, with updated, positive reviews and a fresh look making a solid impression.

➢ Success indicators, such as qualified inquiries and targeted messaging, allow you to refine strategies and ensure that marketing efforts attract serious, well-matched buyers.

➢ If you don't have the qualifications or experience to develop the marketing materials, hire someone who does.

CHAPTER

# CONFIDENTIALITY AND FINDING THE IDEAL BUYER

A common concern amongst business owners is the fear that word will get out that they're selling. It's a legitimate worry. Some might even call it paranoia, and I don't blame them. You may think you can safely discuss your sale plans with a few close friends or family members, but that's a misconception that can lead to major issues. If people—especially in smaller communities—hear that your business is on the market, it can harm your business in ways you may not have anticipated.

Maintaining confidentiality protects your business's value as you move through the sale process. If the wrong people hear about the potential sale, they could start second-guessing your stability and loyalty. I've seen it happen—once employees start worrying about the future, some may begin looking for other opportunities, especially if they fear layoffs or new management.

This can be particularly problematic in smaller businesses with a close-knit team. Imagine you have five or six staff, maybe a few more. If even two or three key team members start looking elsewhere due to job insecurity, it can send a shockwave through your operations. Losing valuable, trained employees disrupts your day-to-day and begins to chip away at your business's value. Suddenly, a prospective buyer might see a company with a dwindling, uneasy workforce rather than a well-oiled machine ready for a smooth transition.

If your suppliers catch wind that you're selling, they may decide to change their payment terms. You might be used to extended payment terms to manage your cash flow, and suddenly, they demand immediate payment to mitigate their perceived risk. That shift could choke your cash flow right when you need it the most.

Customers, too, may feel uneasy. They could start questioning whether they'll still have warranties, reliable support, or service continuity, and some might even start looking for alternatives. This uncertainty can drive loyal customers away, again impacting the stability and value of your business.

That's why I always recommend only sharing sale information with your spouse or immediate family if they're closely involved in your life and business decisions. Beyond that, it's best to keep discussions strictly with essential parties. It's about safeguarding your business's value, ensuring continuity, and keeping you in the strongest possible position when the right buyer comes along.

## Marketing the Sale Without Giving Away the Secret

A costly mistake is how some sellers—or even their agents—go about advertising. Some real estate agents who handle business sales treat it like selling a property. They'll put a picture of the business right up on a website, almost like a for-sale sign in the window. This approach practically screams, "This business is up for grabs!" Suddenly, staff, customers, suppliers—anyone who comes across that listing—know you're selling, and that knowledge alone can lead to the issues we've discussed: staff insecurity, cash flow issues from suppliers, and customers looking for alternatives.

When I advertise a business for sale, we use a "blind profile." This approach keeps the business's identity hidden while giving interested buyers enough insight to assess if it's something they'd like to pursue. We focus on industry details and key points about the business's strengths without revealing identifying information. We sometimes need to be a bit creative with our descriptions. For example, if the business is a franchise, we might list it as a general business within the relevant industry—without specifying it's a franchise. In high-visibility fields like fast food, professional services, or even more niche areas, we avoid using language or imagery that could inadvertently tip off the business's identity.

When advertising a specialized business, we take extra steps to ensure confidentiality. For example, if the business is a high-end furniture store, we might display a generic photo of a retail furniture environment rather than something recognizable. We avoid any language or marketing imagery the business may have previously used in its promotions. These tailored approaches allow us to communicate essential details while protecting your business's identity until the right buyer is ready to move forward.

## *Screening Qualified Buyers in Three Steps*

Before any potential buyer can examine your business in more detail, they need to undergo a three-part screening. This begins with signing a non-disclosure agreement (NDA) that legally binds them to confidentiality. The agreement ensures they won't disclose sensitive information about your business to others.

Beyond the NDA, we also require potential buyers to share their work history, education, and financial background. This second screening layer helps us assess whether they have the necessary experience and understanding to operate a business like yours. Finally, we review their financial history to confirm they have the personal equity to proceed with a transaction.

This three-step approach helps prevent tire-kickers—those who may inquire out of curiosity but lack the resources or expertise to make a legitimate offer. When we filter inquiries this way, we maintain control and only share your sensitive information with vetted individuals who can make a serious offer.

A tightly controlled, discreet process helps preserve what you've worked so hard to build, shielding you from unnecessary disruptions and ensuring the transition to a new owner happens smoothly and strategically. Whether protecting your relationships with employees, securing vendor trust, or maintaining customer loyalty, every measure we take to keep your sale confidential adds to your business's long-term health and value. The goal is to find the right fit while safeguarding what matters most to you.

It is important to note that while confidentiality is paramount in my world, there is only so much I can do to manage this. For example, I cannot stop you and your partner from talking about the process at the dinner table with the kids around. The next day, your children talk about what they heard to their friends at school. Their friends now go home to tell their parents what they heard at school. And the next thing you know, the word is out. It is literally that simple, and yes, this actually happened. So please be very cautious about who is around when discussing the possibility of selling your business.

# KEY TAKEAWAYS

➢ Keeping your business sale confidential avoids disrupting employee morale, supplier terms, and customer loyalty, all of which can impact its value.

➢ Limiting disclosure of your sale plans to only essential parties—ideally, immediate family or key decision-makers—is vital to protecting business continuity.

➢ Advertising your business through a "blind profile" helps attract qualified buyers while preserving confidentiality and preventing leaks that could harm your business's operations and reputation.

➢ Screening potential buyers through NDAs, background checks, and financial assessments ensures that only serious, qualified individuals can access your business's sensitive information.

➢ Maintaining a discreet, structured sale process can secure the right buyer and protect the relationships that make your business valuable.

➢ Remember, "loose lips sink ships." Know who's within earshot of your conversations about selling your business.

CHAPTER

# BUYING A BUSINESS

By now, you may be wondering, "Why is there so much information relating to buying a business in a book about selling a business?" While it is true, there's a lot of preparation and work that needs to be done when selling your business. The fact of the matter is that understanding your prospective buyer - their limitations, motivations, and qualifications needed to purchase and build upon your business successfully - is paramount to your success in this endeavour.

One of the biggest, yet often unasked, questions buyers have when entering the market is: *"What can I actually afford to buy?"* This is especially common with first-time buyers. They are full of ambition but have little understanding of what's realistic within their financial reach. And it isn't necessarily their fault. Many people are new to this world and are unaware of the financial benchmarks they should aim for.

One reason buyers don't know what they can afford is the crazy stories circulating on the internet about buying a business with no money down. For whatever reason, I get contacted semi-regularly by people trying to get on this bandwagon. Allow me to set the record straight. I do not and will not advise any business owner to sell their business for no money down. The whole notion is preposterous!

Now, let's get back to reality. I'm not usually a big fan of rules of thumb, but this one is practical and often very accurate:

**If you're considering buying a business, aim to have between 20% and 50% of the asking price available as liquid assets within three months.**

For example, let's say you're eyeing a business with a $1 million price tag. To realistically afford it, you'd need anywhere from $200,000 to $500,000 in liquid assets—cash in the bank or other quickly accessible funds. If you only have $25,000 or $50,000 to your name, that million-dollar dream business is, frankly, out of reach for now.

Most people don't start with a million-dollar budget. Instead, they work their way up. And that's perfectly okay! A $100,000 business might be where many buyers begin their entrepreneurial journey. From there, they can grow it, develop it over five or ten years, and eventually sell it to step into something bigger that aligns with their longer-term dreams.

This knowledge is your advantage as a seller. When you understand the financial parameters buyers are working within, you can position your business to attract serious and capable buyers. Setting a realistic asking price and preparing your business for the market with this in mind helps ensure you connect with the right audience—those who can afford to buy and are ready to grow what you've built.

## Understanding the Different Types of Buyers

Here are the main types of buyers that could be interested in your business. Knowing which type of buyer would be a good fit for your business is important, so you are prepared to market to and negotiate appropriately with them.

**Corporate buyers** are companies or organizations that acquire other businesses to achieve strategic goals, such as expanding market share, gaining access to new technologies or products, entering new markets, or improving operational efficiencies. Unlike individual or financial buyers, corporate buyers are motivated by strategic synergies rather than primarily by financial returns. You need to be aware of the cultural fit in this situation. While they may be willing to pay a premium for the right business, if their culture is drastically different from yours, this could spell disaster for your employees after closing.

**Employee Share Ownership Plan (ESOP)** is a flexible, customizable solution for transferring business ownership to employees while preserving the company's legacy, culture, and independence. With proper legal, financial, and tax planning, it can be a win-win for both the exiting owner and the employees—particularly in the small to mid-sized business landscape.

**Family offices** are private wealth management advisory firms established by affluent individuals or families. They provide a range of personalized financial, investment, and administrative services. Their purpose is to manage high-net-worth families' wealth, investments, and personal affairs, often across multiple generations. Often, these investors will want to hold onto the business they buy for the long term and are looking for businesses that complement their existing portfolio.

**First-time entrepreneurs** are individuals who are starting or running their first business venture. They often come from diverse backgrounds, such as corporate careers, academic environments, or unrelated fields. They are motivated by a desire for independence, innovation, or the opportunity to solve a problem in the marketplace. These buyers will often require more education and hand-holding through the acquisition process.

**Financial buyers** are individuals or entities (such as a private equity firm, investment fund, or high-net-worth individual) that purchase businesses primarily to achieve financial returns. Unlike corporate buyers, financial buyers focus on the profitability, cash flow, and potential for growth of the target business rather than strategic integration into their existing operations. Most of them understand that there's more to a business than just its numbers. However, their focus is on the top and bottom lines.

**Foreign investors** are individuals, companies, or entities based in one country investing capital in businesses, projects, or assets in another country. Their investments can take various forms, such as acquiring businesses, buying real estate, purchasing stocks or bonds, or funding large infrastructure projects. The goals of foreign investors can range from financial returns to gaining access to new markets, resources, or technologies. Working with these buyers can be challenging as more government red tape can be involved.

**Immigrant entrepreneurs** are the same as first-time entrepreneurs, serial entrepreneurs, turnaround entrepreneurs, etc., but they are citizens of another country and could be looking to buy your business to gain citizenship. Similarly, working with these buyers can be challenging as more government red tape can be involved.

**Management buy-out (MBO) teams** occur when the existing management team of a company purchases the business, either outright or by acquiring a controlling stake, often with external financing. This allows the management team to become the owners of the company they already run. MBOs are a common way for businesses to transition ownership, especially in cases where the current owner wants to retire or divest.

**Private equity groups (PEGs)** are investment management companies that provide financial backing and invest in private companies, often by acquiring or buying a controlling interest in those businesses. These firms typically use pooled funds from institutional investors and high-net-worth individuals to pursue these investments. Most of these entities prefer to resell the businesses they buy within 3 to 7 years.

**Search funders** are entrepreneurs or investors who raise capital from multiple high-net-worth relationships to acquire and operate a business, typically a small to medium-sized enterprise (SME). The process often involves finding an established, profitable company to purchase, taking over management, and working to grow and improve the business over time. Each investor will likely require separate due diligence to approve their participation in the acquisition. As such, working with these buyers can be prolonged and arduous. However, they can also be a good fit for many businesses.

**Serial entrepreneurs** start, run, and often exit multiple businesses or ventures over their careers. Unlike traditional entrepreneurs who may focus on growing a single business over the long term, serial entrepreneurs thrive on building, scaling, and transitioning between multiple ventures. They often sell their successful businesses to pursue new opportunities, leveraging their previous experiences and networks to increase their chances of success in future endeavors.

**Strategic buyers** are companies or entities that acquire another business primarily to achieve long-term strategic goals, such as expanding market presence, integrating supply chains, enhancing product or service offerings, or gaining access to new technology or intellectual property. Unlike financial buyers, who focus primarily on return on investment (ROI), strategic buyers aim to create value through synergies and alignment with their existing operations.

**Turnaround entrepreneurs** thrive on identifying underperforming or struggling businesses, acquiring them at a reduced price, and implementing strategies to restore profitability and operational efficiency.

Having just read through the different buyer types, which one do you think would be a good fit to take over your business, and why? If you're able to answer those questions, you're in a good position to begin the sales process.

### The Passive Income Myth

I always hear it: *"Can you help me find a business where I don't actually have to work, and it just makes me money?"* Who wouldn't want that? But let me tell you, if I had a whole bunch of businesses for sale that were completely hands-off and generated reliable passive income, I probably wouldn't be selling them to you. I'd be buying them myself!

Those opportunities do exist, but they are rare. More often than not, when you're looking for a business that can run itself, you're stepping into a much higher price range—typically in the $3 to $5 million range and up. These businesses have management teams in place and are structured more like investments than owner-operated ventures.

For the majority of buyers, especially those looking at businesses under $2 million, the expectation of passive income isn't realistic. If you're buying a business in this range, you'll likely need to be involved in the daily operations. You won't just be working *on* the business; you'll be working *in* it to keep things running smoothly and to drive growth.

This misconception often stems from the allure of passive income in other areas, like real estate. Owning rental properties, for instance, can involve hiring property managers to handle the day-to-day work. But businesses are different. They're dynamic and require more involvement if you genuinely want to succeed.

Understanding the different buyer types and their expectations can help you better position your business for sale. If your business is well-structured, with systems in place and a solid management team, you're offering a rare opportunity likely to command a premium price. On the other hand, if your business requires hands-on involvement, being upfront about this reality will attract buyers who are prepared for the challenge and willing to roll up their sleeves.

### The Hidden Costs Buyers Overlook

Another set of misconceptions revolves around the hidden costs and logistics of owning a business after the sale is finalized. Many buyers focus solely on the purchase price, overlooking the expenses they'll face once they take ownership. As a seller, you should understand these factors so you can prepare for and address buyer concerns. These overlooked costs often include:

- ❖ **Deposits for Operational Accounts**: Buyers may need to pay deposits for utilities like heat, hydro, internet, and phone systems. They'll also need to cover setup costs for essential business systems, such as point-of-sale (POS) platforms.
- ❖ **First and Last Month's Rent**: If the business operates in a leased space, buyers must budget for rental deposits, which can be substantial depending on the property.
- ❖ **Franchise Fees and Training Costs**: If your business is part of a franchise, buyers might face costs for a new franchise license, onboarding fees, and mandatory training sessions.
- ❖ **License Transfers and Vehicle Compliance**: Businesses requiring specific government, municipal, or regulatory licenses will involve transfer fees and potentially lengthy processing times. For companies with vehicles, buyers may need to pay for inspections and ensure compliance with safety regulations, even if the vehicles pass initial checks.

When I work with buyers, I always advise them to budget for professional fees like accountant reviews, legal counsel, and other necessary advisors. As another practical rule of thumb:

- **For deals under $1 million**, buyers should allocate about $5,000 to $10,000 for these expenses.
- **For deals over $1 million**, those fees will naturally increase. The larger and more complex the deal, the more time professionals will need to spend reviewing and negotiating, which drives up their fees.

One of the benefits of using my services is that I can reduce the costs for both the accountants and lawyers and for both you and the buyer. Between the work being done to value and market the business, I've generally collected about 90% to 95% of the needed due diligence information. Also, by using my services to negotiate an offer to purchase, you can save on some legal fees - if you're not able to come to acceptable terms in that process, then there's no use in paying a lawyer $300 to $500+/hour to try and negotiate this. Their fees are due regardless of the outcome, whereas mine are only due if/when the deal closes and you get paid.

The most common pitfall buyers face is underestimating the expenses of purchasing and operating a business. It's easy to think, *"I'll make it work"* or *"I'll only need three months of cash flow to get by,"* when in reality, you might need six months—or more—to stabilize operations. This kind of miscalculation can quickly set them up for financial strain and jeopardize the business.

Remember when we discussed working capital a little bit ago? It comes into play again here. One of the first things I stress to buyers is having enough working capital in the business to support operations during the transition period. Working capital is the financial cushion that keeps the lights on, pays the bills, and compensates employees until the business generates a steady cash flow.

This steady cash flow can be another hidden challenge for businesses in industries like construction or trade services. In many cases, these businesses operate on delayed payment cycles, with receivables arriving 60, 90, or even 180 days after work is completed. Buyers stepping into these industries need a plan for managing operating costs during those gaps. That means securing access to a line of credit or other financing to cover wages, supplies, and overhead until revenue catches up. Sellers can entertain more serious buyers by presenting a clear cash flow history and actionable strategies for navigating these challenges. One of the greatest advantages you can offer as a seller is transparency.

## *Finding the Right Business to Buy*

When first-time buyers ask me what type of business they should buy, the answer often lies in their own experience and skills. It's common to underestimate just how transferable their background can be! For example:

- **Retail Experience**: Knowledge gained in one retail niche often translates well to others, as the fundamentals of managing inventory, customer service, and sales are similar across different sectors.
- **Office Administration or Warehouse Backgrounds**: These can provide a strong foundation for transitioning into businesses that require operational oversight, logistics, or supply chain management.

Part of your role as a seller is to help buyers connect the dots between their talents and the opportunities your business offers. By framing your business as approachable and emphasizing its scalability or potential, you make it easier for people to envision themselves stepping into your shoes and thriving.

Of course, transferable skills can only take someone so far. A buyer's willingness to learn is just as important. Some buyers might find themselves drawn to industries they've admired or had a passion for earlier in life. While they may not have worked in that field for decades—or ever—the desire to learn and adapt can help them succeed.

The best advice I can give anyone considering buying a business is this: **focus on opportunities that make sense for you.** Too often, buyers inquire about businesses that don't align with their experience, interests, or financial capacity. They may be hoping to "get on the radar" of brokers or sellers, but these mismatched inquiries rarely go anywhere. For sellers, this can waste time and create unnecessary back-and-forth. For buyers, it can damage credibility and limit future opportunities.

I always advise buyers: *Don't reach out unless you're serious.* That means inquiring only when you've done your homework and the business aligns with your goals, expertise, and budget. Sellers respect buyers who come prepared and recognize the fit between what the business offers and what they bring to the table.

As a seller, make sure your messaging is clear, concise, and accurately represents the business. When you articulate what's required for success— experience in a specific industry, financial benchmarks, or particular skills—you'll entice qualified buyers who are ready to take the next step.

## KEY TAKEAWAYS

➤ Buyers should realistically assess their financial capacity before pursuing a business, aiming to have 20% to 50% of the asking price in liquid assets.

➤ The expectation of passive income is often misplaced; most businesses under $2 million require hands-on involvement, and sellers should communicate operational realities to attract the right buyers.

➤ Hidden costs such as utility deposits, rent, franchise fees, and professional services often surprise buyers; sellers can build trust by transparently addressing these post-purchase expenses.

➤ Buyers thrive when they align opportunities with their skills and experience.

➤ Prepared buyers with clear goals, research, and serious inquiries save time for both parties, while clear, detailed listings from sellers attract qualified, motivated buyers.

➤ Understanding who the most likely buyer is for your business will better prepare you for the selling, marketing, and negotiating process.

➤ My services will save you money on your closing costs.

CHAPTER

# AFTER SELLING
# YOUR BUSINESS

## *It's Not Goodbye Just Yet...*

Selling your business is a monumental achievement. However, it's not as simple as signing the papers and walking away into the sunset. Many business owners assume that they can pack their bags, travel the globe, and leave their business behind once the deal is finalized. While that scenario is possible, it's the exception, not the rule.

I once knew a business owner who sold his company to a friend of mine. Two weeks after the sale, the seller hopped on his plane and started flying around the world, living his dream of ultimate freedom. The buyer hardly heard from him again. That story might sound appealing, but for the vast majority of business sales I've facilitated, there's been a much more extended transition period. Whether it's a few weeks, months, or even longer, you should expect to be involved post-sale to oversee a smooth transfer of operations, preserve the business's reputation, and protect the relationships you've built with customers, employees, and suppliers.

Conversely, another business owner's identity was so tied to his business that even after the two-year transition period was completed, they kept coming to work. One day, the new owner pulled them aside and asked them to stop coming in, stating that the staff, customers, etc., needed to know that the buyer was the boss now and not the previous owner.

You can't disappear overnight if you've been the face and/or name of the business, the one closing deals, managing sales, or representing the company in public-facing roles. During this transition, you'll likely work side by side with the new owner. Your role is to provide a personal introduction to the people who rely on your business and the processes and operations that make it tick. Imagine yourself in those initial meetings saying, "This is the new person you'll be working with, and I have complete confidence in them." Your endorsement can go a long way in maintaining trust and stability.

For the first few weeks—or even months—you might need to attend most if not all, key handover interactions. These could include meetings with major clients, vendors, or employees, where your presence helps reassure everyone that the business is in good hands. You'll gradually phase yourself out once the buyer becomes more comfortable and confident in their role. Think of it like teaching someone to ride a bike: at first, you're holding on tightly, running alongside them. Then, as they gain their balance, you let go—allowing them to ride solo while you step back.

If you're selling to a competitor or someone with substantial industry experience, their familiarity with the business model and industry processes may significantly shorten the transition period. In these cases, your role might be limited to helping them understand specific systems or structures unique to your business. Once they've grasped those essentials, you can pursue your post-sale plans.

On the other hand, if the buyer is new to the industry, your involvement is likely to be longer. I've worked with sellers who signed contracts to stay on for up to two years. These extended arrangements can also occur in scenarios where government licensing is involved. In such cases, the buyer might not be able to operate fully until their licensing is approved, leaving the seller technically responsible for the business in the meantime. Even in these longer-term scenarios, your role isn't necessarily hands-on. You may not need to be involved in the day-to-day operations, but you still have a responsibility to oversee the transition and ensure that everything runs smoothly.

## THE VALUE OF OFFERING A TRANSITION PERIOD

Whether the transition period is initiated by the seller or requested by the buyer, it can significantly influence how attractive your business appears in the market. Buyers often seek reassurance that they won't be left adrift once the sale is complete, especially if the business relies heavily on the seller's expertise or relationships.

There are situations where offering transition support isn't feasible—perhaps the seller is facing serious health issues or has already passed away. In these cases, the lack of direction can place the business in what we call a "distressed" state. While some buyers specifically look for such opportunities, most prefer businesses where the seller is available to provide guidance. A clear willingness to offer a transition period makes the business more appealing and easier to sell at a premium value.

## *The Business Broker's Role Post-Sale*

Once the sale of a business is finalized, my job as a business broker typically becomes less hands-on. That said, I remain available to step in if needed. One of the ways I support both parties post-sale is by acting as a mediator. Sometimes, misunderstandings or disputes arise between the buyer and the seller. For example, a buyer might feel the seller isn't fulfilling certain post-sale obligations, or the seller may think the buyer is misinterpreting the terms of the agreement. In such cases, I can help clarify the situation, avoiding the need for legal action.

In addition to mediation, I often assist with logistical or administrative follow-ups. Buyers or sellers may misplace important documents—ownership papers, manuals, insurance policies, or other materials. Since I've collected and organized much of this documentation throughout the sale process, I can quickly retrieve and share what's needed to resolve the issue.

While my involvement post-sale is far less intensive than during the negotiation and transaction phases, my continued availability provides an added layer of reassurance. It's part of my ongoing commitment to ensure both parties' success in closing the deal and in the transition that follows.

## *Tips for a Seamless Handover*

One of the most practical tips I give sellers is creating detailed manuals and documentation. These resources serve as a guide for the new owner and help reduce the risk of confusion or resistance from staff. For example, if your business has a team of 10 to 20 employees handling various roles, it's essential to document what each position entails. This is particularly important in businesses where staff may have worn multiple hats over the years.

If a situation arises after the sale where an employee says, "That's not part of my job," the new owner can refer to your documentation and say, "Actually, according to this manual, you've been handling this task for 19 years." Having this kind of backup can prevent unnecessary conflicts and give the buyer confidence in managing the team.

Detailed documentation should cover every aspect of your operations—sales processes, manufacturing workflows, customer service protocols, or anything else specific to your business—the more comprehensive the materials, the better.

To preserve your business legacy, approach the relationship with the buyer as a partnership. Treat them as you would a trusted colleague or even a family member. Your shared goal is the same: for the business to thrive. A big part of this involves sharing your "secret sauce." Whether it's how you've managed challenging suppliers, handled demanding customers, or led your team through growth and change, this insider knowledge can be invaluable to the new owner. These are the insights they need to succeed.

If seller financing is part of the deal, your willingness to guide and support the buyer becomes even more critical. Their success directly impacts their ability to meet their financial obligations to you. A struggling buyer could result in missed payments or financial strain, whereas a thriving buyer creates a smooth transition and peace of mind for all parties.

Your effort in this final stage of the journey can ensure that the business continues to flourish and that you step away with confidence, knowing you've done everything possible to secure the future of what you built.

# KEY TAKEAWAYS

➢ Selling your business often requires a transition period where you stay involved to facilitate a smooth handover and maintain trust with clients, employees, and suppliers.

➢ Tailored involvement during the transition depends on the buyer's industry experience, ranging from hands-on support to a more advisory role.

➢ A clearly defined transition period enhances the business's market appeal, reassuring buyers and potentially increasing its value. Have a serious conversation with yourself and the prospective buyer, and set clear expectations for this.

➢ Detailed manuals and documentation can prevent operational confusion, foster team cohesion, and give the new owner confidence in managing the business.

➢ Treat the buyer as a partner, sharing insider knowledge and maintaining a collaborative approach to ensure the business's ongoing success and protect its legacy.

# THE 30 ROLES OF A BUSINESS BROKER

Many owners wonder if they should sell their business themselves. After all, who knows your business better than you do? Over the years, I've seen people attempt to handle the sale on their own, only to find themselves overwhelmed by the process and leaving money—or opportunities—on the table.

As a business broker, I wear many hats (and I'm not just talking about my closet full of them, which I've become known for). When I sat down to think about my roles during a business sale, I came up with roughly 30 distinct responsibilities. They are tasks I perform daily, both as a business broker and as an owner of my office in Kingston. That dual role gives me a unique perspective, as I understand firsthand the challenges business owners face.

## THE 30 ROLES OF A BUSINESS BROKER

BUSINESS BROKER

**1. Administrator**
**2. Support Staff**
**3. Human Resources**
**4. Researcher**
**5. Advertising / Marketing Manager**
**6. Content writer**
**7. Direct Mail Manager**
**8. Computer Support**
**9. Software Trainer**
**10. Controller / Bookkeeper**
**11. Tax coordinator**
12. Educator
13. Counselor / Therapist
14. Industrial Psychologist
15. Insurance Coordinator
16. Exit / Estate Planner / Manager
17. Due Diligence Manager
18. Legal Coordinator
19. Accounting Coordinator
20. Public Relations
21. Business Broker / Salesperson / Real Estate Broker
22. Negotiator / Mediator
23. Business Analyst
24. Business Valuator

MY OWN BUSINESS

1. **Administrator**
2. **Support Staff**
3. **Human Resources**
4. **Researcher**
5. **Advertising / Marketing Manager**
6. **Content writer**
7. **Direct Mail Manager**
8. **Computer Support**
9. **Software Trainer**
10. **Controller / Bookkeeper**
11. **Tax Coordinator**
12. Student
13. Volunteer
14. Seminar Coordinator / Presenter
15. Recruiter
16. Mentor
17. Sales Manager

The **bold** roles indicate that I perform them both as a broker working with clients and as a business owner.

Initially, I act as a business consultant and valuator. My first task is helping the business owner understand the market value of their business—not what they hope it's worth but what the market is likely to pay for it. This involves extensive research, financial analysis, and sometimes even software consulting to connect all the moving parts of the business.

I dig into cash flows, balance sheets, and inventory management systems, often going back 24 months of monthly balance sheets to identify trends and seasonality and 5 years for the overall financial health of the business. This phase alone can take months to complete, and it requires me to play the roles of an accountant, bookkeeper, market researcher, buyer, and valuator.

As the process continues, a few roles stand out as the most crucial to ensuring a smooth sale. At the top of the list are responsibilities that focus on organization and preparation.

## Administrator and HR Specialist

One of my primary responsibilities is acting as an administrator or HR person for the business. I help owners organize their internal systems, which is no small task. For instance, I make sure vehicle ownership is up to date, insurance policies are current, and WSIB statements and claims are in order. I also work with clients to ensure employee files are complete and accurate.

## Marketing and Packaging

Marketing the business consists of creating unique, customized content that highlights the business's strengths while making it appealing to prospective buyers. I help package the business so buyers can imagine themselves stepping into the owner's shoes and confidently taking over operations. This also includes addressing the business's shortcomings and liabilities. Prospective buyers need to know about these. It's better to address them early so they don't become deal breakers later.

## VETTING PROSPECTIVE BUYERS

Not every interested party is a good fit, and it's my responsibility to make the right match. I evaluate buyers to determine their financial capacity, operational expertise, and long-term interest in the business. This step helps save business owners from wasting time with unqualified buyers.

## PREPARING FOR DUE DILIGENCE

Due diligence is one of the most intense phases of a business sale. Buyers and their advisors will comb through your business to check that everything is in order, from financials to operations. To make sure we're ready, I guide my clients through a series of structured steps. For example, I have six to eight templated emails prepared, tailored to the nature of the business, that request specific pieces of information. These emails outline everything I'll need initially, from employee records to operational documents, and set the stage for additional requests down the line. As I work with you to prepare your business for market, this information will typically represent approximately 90% or more of the information needed for the due diligence process. Having this ready in advance will expedite that process and instill confidence in the buyer(s) and bank(s) that you're ready to sell your business and that the information they're getting is accurate.

## *Rubber Meets the Road*

Unfortunately, there are times when accepted offers fail to make it past the due diligence period to successfully transition ownership of the business. This can happen for all kinds of reasons. The top four are:

- Banks aren't able/willing to fund the deal.
- Landlords/franchisors aren't willing to accept the new buyer or let the current owner out of the contract.
- Lawyers aren't able to reach an agreement on the drafting of the final documentation.
- Information is discovered that suggests the business isn't as good of a fit as they once thought.

Of course, there are other reasons, but those are the main ones that occur most often. Sometimes, when prospective buyers review your internal records, they might discover that your client list has a high level of churn, or it's too concentrated for their preference. Maybe your equipment or vehicle maintenance records suggest that most of your assets are held together with duct tape and super glue, and they would need to invest more money than they want to or have to bring your equipment up to standards. Or, possibly, your workplace safety history is poor, which can result in higher than desired employee benefits, WSIB, and other associated costs.

Even though I do as much diligence as possible to ensure that any accepted offer meets the criteria for all parties involved, sometimes there are requirements in their world that I cannot account for. Please don't be afraid to tell me about anything like the above, as I need to know about these details before we go to market so that I can address them properly in the marketing collateral. Prospective buyers need to be aware of them early on, so they're less likely to kill your deal during the due diligence stage. Let's find out early on if anything will scare a prospective buyer away, before accountants and lawyers start charging you their hourly rates to begin working on a deal that won't close.

The good news is that even if a deal dies during the due diligence period, my continued marketing efforts may still generate interest in your business, allowing us to restart the negotiation process with another buyer.

## When Going Solo Gets Overwhelming

It's not uncommon for business owners to attempt selling their business on their own. They dive in with enthusiasm, trying to connect with a few potential buyers, only to hit a point where they realize they're in over their heads. Often, the trigger is a simple yet frustrating fact: **they don't know what they don't know.** They find the process consuming more of their time than they ever imagined. Inquiries pour in, and without experience managing them, they don't know when to stop, how much information to share, or when to share it. Every moment spent responding to buyer questions or handling due diligence is a moment taken away from running the business effectively. This adds stress and can hurt the business's performance, which is the last thing you want when trying to sell. That's usually when I get the call.

I'm currently working with a client who started trying to sell their business independently. They approached three or four potential buyers, but those discussions went nowhere. Eventually, they realized they needed professional help and reached out to me.

Fast forward to today, and we've had their business on the market for less than two months. Not only do we have an initial offer on the table, but there's also a second buyer waiting in the wings. This didn't happen by accident; it resulted from a well-structured, professional approach to continuously marketing the business. By front-loading the necessary work—organizing documents, setting up a clear process, and establishing protocols for sharing information—we made the workload much lighter for the seller.

## *A Trusted Partner*

One of the most significant roles I play as a business broker is that of a trusted confidant and ally to the business owner. I often joke that working with a business owner is like dating because the level of communication is so constant. From the moment we begin, there's a steady flow of texts, emails, and phone calls. This communication is especially frequent for the first three to six months as we prepare the business for sale, navigate early inquiries, and begin negotiations.

By the time we're in the thick of negotiations or the due diligence process, I have a comprehensive picture of what matters most to you, the owner. This allows me to represent your interests effectively and negotiate in a way that aligns with your priorities. My role is to present your story in the best possible light, whether we're addressing concerns from a buyer or overcoming financial, leasing, and/or due diligence hurdles.

Throughout the sale, business owners share more than just their business's financial and operational details. They share their personal stories, struggles, and even the occasional "deep, dark secrets" from their journey. This level of trust is an integral part of the relationship we build, and it is one of the most rewarding parts of being a broker. Selling a business is deeply personal, and I take the responsibility of being a confidant to the owner during this pivotal moment in their life very seriously.

# KEY TAKEAWAYS

➢ Selling a business is far more complex than most owners anticipate. It requires expertise in valuation, marketing, vetting buyers, and preparing for due diligence. A professional broker simplifies the steps and maximizes opportunities.

➢ A broker's roles include technical responsibilities like financial analysis and marketing and organizational support, such as preparing documents, ensuring compliance, and streamlining due diligence.

➢ The ability to present a business effectively involves crafting a compelling narrative that resonates with buyers and makes them feel confident about taking over operations.

➢ I need to know your business's "good, bad, and ugly" sides to help you best.

➢ Many owners who attempt to sell on their own quickly become overwhelmed, often realizing too late that they lack the time, experience, and knowledge to navigate the process efficiently.

➢ Beyond technical expertise, a broker serves as a trusted partner, building a deep relationship with the owner to understand their priorities and guide them through one of the most significant transitions of their life.

# Bonus Chapter

# CONVERSATION WITH GRANT MELLOW

In this conversation, Jim Nairn sits down with business coach Grant Mellow, who specializes in helping business owners strengthen their operations, increase profitability, and position their companies for a successful exit. Grant shares a powerful success story of a business that went from struggling to survive to helping them scale to sell for $14 million in just six years. Through precise financial tracking, leadership alignment, and strategic operational improvements, Grant helped transform the business into an attractive acquisition target. This interview provides valuable insights into what it takes to prepare a business for sale and why taking early action is crucial for any owner looking to exit successfully.

—

**Jim Nairn**: *Grant, you have been a long-time friend of mine (a little over 10 years now). You are a business coach who helps business brokers strengthen their clients' businesses to prepare them for sale. Tell us about your work.*

**Grant Mellow:** I guide business owners to maximize their value and have a rewarding exit, leaving a personally meaningful legacy. People often don't hit the number they want or see an opportunity to grow the business more, and that's where we start. They may be ready now or in a few years, but the time to get started is *now.*

**Jim Nairn:** *Do you have a success story about one of the clients you have helped?*

**Grant Mellow:** Yes. This business started small and became a high-value, multi-million-dollar sale in a few years. In this case, the business was in a really strong professional services market, with a great niche and a unique approach. The company had a solid reputation and a steady stream of clients, but despite strong demand, it was struggling. Growth came at a cost—profits were weak, financial tracking was unreliable, and senior leadership couldn't agree on a clear direction.

We started with a lot of chaos. They had tried many different approaches, and we just had to get really focused on bringing order to things before we could get into scaling. The first step for me is always to clarify "what are we making?" You can't have two or three different visions on the table. We had to get it down to one aligned set of priorities. Once we had the priorities set for the new vision, we established a solid financial tracking system. Then we had good, accurate numbers so we could make decisions based on data rather than "gut" instinct. Compliance measures were tightened so that we consistently executed our system, and then our key performance indicators showed us which aspects of the system were delivering results and which weren't.

The numbers started turning out reasonably well, but we had one more fundamental challenge to overcome: one of the senior leaders remained resistant to the agreed priorities, and they continued pushing in a different direction than the rest of the team. Their reluctance to align caused chaos and friction. So, after a lot of careful evaluation, we made the tough decision to remove them from the company so we could build momentum. Once that was done, the leadership was fully aligned.

The next challenge was reducing the owner's day-to-day involvement in operations. They were still the key decision-maker and lacked time to focus on growth. So, we refined internal systems to ensure that daily decision-making was distributed throughout the team and processes were implemented that allowed the new processes to be easily replicable. We applied some technology to help with that because it didn't take a person to manage it.

Then, it was just about getting the right people in place. We built a good framework that allowed potential issues to be flagged before they became bigger problems and caused more chaos. Some team members worked well under that new system, while others struggled. In the end, we had to replace a couple of them. They were good people but didn't fit into that system. Once we got through that, we were ready for the next steps, and the business could grow and scale.

The third step was readiness for sale. By that point, we had good financials, the leadership was aligned, operations were streamlined, and scalability was in place. A key indicator of this was that the owner wasn't trapped in the daily grind anymore—they were actually working on building the business.

At this point, the business started attracting the attention of some big players. Beyond the strength of the refined systems, stable operations, and untapped potential they saw, they also liked this business's unique service approach. They realized they could apply and leverage that through their other systems, significantly increasing the company's value.

**Jim Nairn:** *What was it like when you had to remove one of the senior leaders from the company?*

**Grant Mellow:** It's never easy because everybody thinks they bring value. Naturally, they see it from their own perspective. However, aligning the owners is the number one item when I work with businesses. And if we can't accomplish that, we either have to pick one, or there's no point in working with them. In this business, one person clearly held the cards in terms of ownership—they had the majority ownership—and their strategy was solid, so that's what we went with. It's not an easy step for many people because, like I said, everyone thinks they're bringing value to the table. But it must be done because we can't have conflicting priorities from the executive level.

**Jim Nairn:** *What about when it came down to the staff? How did you handle them?*

**Grant Mellow:** The staff is interesting. If you keep changing people without establishing order, it's hard to tell whether the staff is actually the problem or not—whether they fit or not. Once we have the data and the system(s) in place, we can see if they follow it. Then, we know who fits and who doesn't. As I said, they're all good people. It's not an issue of that. It's a matter of whether they fit into this new service model that we're applying. Once that fit is refined and is running smoothly, some people start to feel that they don't fit anymore. So sometimes, it's actually a relief for them to move on to something more personally rewarding.

**Jim Nairn:** *How were the owner and staff changes received by the people staying in the company?*

**Grant Mellow:** Everyone feels the chaos produced by people who don't fit. The team wants to play with people who align with the company's purpose and value. So, it was actually a relief to most people.

**Jim Nairn:** *How did you start working with this company?*

**Grant Mellow:** This business was a referral from someone I was working with. They recognized that the business was struggling in certain areas and not executing its vision. Once it hit a certain size and presence in the market, it became a prime target for being acquired by the bigger players. After six years of working with me, it sold for around $14 million, and when we started, it was only worth whatever it could get for its assets!

Find Grant Mellow at https://www.linkedin.com/in/grantmellow/

## Grant Mellow – Business Coach, GDM Business Coaching

Grant guides business owners to scale with structure, reduce chaos, and prepare for a high-value exit. As the former COO of a national business brokerage, he brings insight into what makes a business valuable—and what holds it back.

With over 21 years of experience, Grant works with owners at or near capacity, helping them evolve their leadership, build routines that reduce dependency, and grow strong, profitable teams. He has worked closely with professional service firms—including bookkeeping businesses—to move from operator-led to scalable and strategic.

Whether your goal is stability, freedom, or preparing your business for sale, Grant's practical coaching helps you get stronger today, so you can be extraordinary tomorrow.

# Epilogue

*"If you think it's expensive to hire a professional to
do the job, wait until you hire an amateur."*
– Red Adair

First of all—congratulations! You've just been given the knowledge you need to get ready to sell your business. Of course, there's still more to learn, but you've taken a significant step forward in this process. You're now better informed and far ahead of the countless business owners who refuse to put in the time to prepare for a sale properly. You now know what the market is looking for, what buyers value, and how to approach the process with your eyes wide open. That alone puts you in a stronger position than most.

Please don't follow the masses and try to shortcut the proven process that has helped so many others achieve their goals. Don't sit on your laurels and do nothing, or worse, try to sell your business entirely on your own. That's how hundreds of thousands—or even millions—of dollars get left on the table. And once that money is gone, it's gone for good. Hopefully, by now, you understand the importance and value of hiring a professional to assist you with this process.

You've built momentum by reading this book, so don't let it go to waste. Take the next step. Book a confidential, no-obligation meeting with me so we can discuss your current situation and your goals:

1. **Meet** – We'll sit down and have a confidential conversation about your business, your numbers, and your objectives.
2. **Assess** – You'll get a clear understanding of where the market sees the value of your business today.
3. **Decide** – Together, we'll determine if now is the right time to sell, or if it's worth growing your business over the next year or two to hit your number.

There's much more to learn about selling a business, and I would be honoured to guide you through the rest of the process. This is why I do what I do. There's nothing more satisfying than seeing my former business owners step into a new chapter of life—free from the everyday stress of running a business—and finally able to focus on what they love to do. It amazes me every single time.

If you're considering buying or selling
a business now—or within the next
three to five years—reach out to me for
a free, confidential consultation.

**jim.nairn@trilliumbusinessbrokerage.com**

# About Jim Nairn, MBA, MCBI, BCA

Even though Jim became aware of the business brokerage world through a friend many years ago while completing his Master's, he has taken to it with great enthusiasm. The idea of helping entrepreneurs through the complex and often emotional process of buying and selling their businesses and witnessing their relief and jubilation upon a successful transition is a driving force for Jim.

It is an unfortunate reality that issues will arise when purchasing or selling a business. Sometimes, these can take a toll on people's emotions and cause extra stress. During those stressful times, Jim encourages his clients to vent about the process and what's going on. After that, he empathetically verifies what is happening and the alternatives/options and offers suggestions on how to best proceed based on his client's goals.

Being an advocate for lifelong learning is a bonus for Jim, as the business brokerage world allows him to continuously build upon his education and experience so that he can better serve his clients' needs. He routinely signs up for additional learning opportunities beyond the numerous courses required to maintain his memberships and designations related to the various industry organizations that he belongs to.

Please do not hesitate to contact Jim for your buying, selling, and/or valuating needs.

# What Jim's Clients Are Saying...

*"We recently purchased a business in the Kingston area. Jim and his team made it a smooth process. Jim ensured that every detail was taken care of throughout the process. We have a great relationship and hope to do business with them again in the future."*
  - Eric Dinelle

*"Thanks to Jim Nairn ... he was professional, courteous, and very knowledgeable. He guided us through the difficult and complicated process of selling a business using his experience and expertise."*
  - Andy Arbuckle

*"I have had an excellent experience working with Jim Nairn. Extremely professional and insightful."*
  - Changlin Wang

*"If you are looking to buy or sell a business, call Jim. He is a man of integrity and will ensure that you get the best deal."*
  - Sanjay Gupta

*"As a commercial and business lender in the area, I have worked with Jim on various projects and opportunities. If you want professional service from a knowledgeable and experienced business broker, Jim is your best choice."*
  - Matt Williams

"*Before I met Jim, I was having a difficult time deciding not only how but whether or not to sell my business at all. It was nice to work with Jim; it felt good having him take the reins on the process for me. Thankfully, after some time, Jim was able to find an appropriate buyer for my business. If you want to sell your business, this is a good avenue.*"

- Mac Gervan

www.ingramcontent.com/pod-product-compliance
Lightning Source LLC
Chambersburg PA
CBHW051317220526
45468CB00004B/1376